Edward Hardy is the pround father of two toddlers: Georgina aged 4 and Devon aged 2. With the onset of parenthood, he noticed a gap on the bookshelves for an amusing yet informative book on having babies, as written from a male perspective, so he wrote it himself. Now in his early thirties, he lives with his family in Ascot, and is a keen cricketer, Star Trek buff, and computer analyst.

WHAT A MARVELLOUS DELIVERY THAT WAS

A Male Spin on Pregnancy and Babies

Edward Hardy

*The antenatal, natal, and postnatal experiences
and observations of a nearly new Millennium man*

Edward Hardy

The Book Guild Ltd
Sussex, England

First published in Great Britain in 2001 by
The Book Guild Ltd
25 High Street,
Lewes, Sussex
BN7 2LU

Typesetting in Times by
SetSystems Ltd, Saffron Walden, Essex

Printed in Great Britain by
Athenaeum Press Ltd, Gateshead

A catalogue record for this book is available from
The British Library

ISBN 1 85776 585 0

CONTENTS

PART 3: Following On

ACKNOWLEDGEMENTS

I am happily indebted to Angela, my wife, for so many things: for marrying me, for having my babies, for generally putting up with me, for making the finest onion bhajis in the Western world, and for countless other enhancements to my life. Without her contribution in the baby-making adventure, this book would never have become even a twinkling in my eye. I am profoundly grateful, and extremely content.

My children, Georgina and Devon, have also enriched my life enormously, and, again, this book could not have happened without their entry into the world. They have been, and continue to be a wonderfully inspiring source of material. Most of all, I am so happy being their father.

I would also like to express my gratitude to Dr. Pete Heywood and to Dr. Hugh Alberti, for reading early extracts from this work, for endorsing the medical aspects contained within, and for laughing in all the right places. Thanks, also, to Cousin Joanie for encouraging me, and for providing me with her womanist critique of my manuscript.

Finally, I would like to dedicate this book to Rachel, a beloved niece. I was so proud when you made me an uncle.

INTRODUCTION

I originally envisaged that this book would be picked up off the shelf mostly by men; after all, it is, essentially, a male perspective on all matters relating to pregnancy, childbirth, and the early development of children.

I have subsequently been led to believe that it will also appeal to women. This change of view was encouraged by a rather dynamic girlfriend of a friend, during a chance conversation in a Mexican restaurant in Virginia Water. Her argument was that my book would give women an insight into how such matters are viewed by the opposite sex. It seems obvious, now, but I was pleasantly surprised to realize, from this, that the simple outpourings of a mere male might indeed be of some interest to females.

Up until that conversation, I had not dared to imagine that my opinions might be read and considered by that half of the population that actually has to undergo all the physical hardships pertaining to pregnancy. After all, women may well feel that they already know more than enough about the subject. I suppose I wanted, from the outset, to assert the fact that men are actually involved in the process, too; but I did not, initially, dream that women might volunteer to be reminded of this.

I hope that I have managed to represent my ideas, opinions, and experiences with an appropriate sensitivity to all parties involved in the pursuit of reproduction. I acknowledge that there will be many differing ways of looking at the issue. Bear in mind that this book is meant to be a personal reflection and not, necessarily, a collection of diverse points of view.

Amusement

After reading a few choice paragraphs from the developing manuscript to my wife, Angela, I realized that my book was destined to be at least mildly amusing, as well as informative. The overall intention was then to help the subject matter along with anecdotes that will make the reader laugh inwardly, rather than burst out into laughter. In order to assess the impact of my attempts at humour, I have frequently consulted with Georgina, my two-year-old daughter. As a general rule, whenever her reaction has been to say 'Ha ha, funny', the joke or anecdote in question has indeed been truly amusing. I hope that I have not been led too far astray in pursuit of a little light-hearted relief to a subject that can sometimes be dealt with too seriously.

Enterprise

One evening during the course of my writing this book, Angela looked over to the word processor in the corner of the room. The monitor was in screen-saver mode, since I had temporarily left the computer idle for more than five minutes. Angela commented that looking into the starfield simulation on the screen gave her the feeling of being on board the *Enterprise*. I was delighted by this reflection, since I consider that any connection between this work and *Star Trek* (specifically *The Next Generation*) is a tremendous compliment.

Angela then added that the movement of the stars on screen did not really suggest warp speed, but more like half impulse power. I could have bridled at this follow-up comment, since it might have implied that I was going rather slowly in compiling this work. I preferred, however, to infer that rather than rushing along at a rate faster than the speed of light, I was instead giving every aspect an appropriate amount of care and consideration.

I like to think that there are a number of links between the subject matter of this book and *Star Trek*. As I see things, having a baby for the first time is very much a journey into *The Undiscovered Country* (the title of the *Star Trek VI* motion picture). Moreover, writing this book is, for me, a similar venture into the unknown, since it is my first work of any notable length.

First Class

When I commenced writing this book, I originally planned a fairly small, pamphlet-style format. Such a work could be likened to a one-day cricket international. Both are designed to provide maximum interest in a short and minimalized context. As the manuscript grew, I began to realize that I had far too many ideas and experiences to be compressed into a short booklet. In this respect, I prefer to think of this work in terms of a test match. Unlike the shortened form of the game, the test match is the ultimate challenge, the proper forum for a serious interplay of diverse skills and experiences. Likewise, this book has grown and grown so much that it has taken on a much more comprehensive range of ideas and subjects relating to the overall theme.

References to cricket will pop up, from time to time, throughout the book. I make no apologies for bringing cricket onto the field of play. I trust, simply, that the extra topics covered will increase the enjoyment gained from the reading of my humble offering.

Admirers of Richie Benaud will have instantly recognized the source of the book's title. I regard Richie as the master of both the spoken and written commentary. Probably his greatest skill is the ability to express himself in an extremely concise manner. I can but hope that a few of my sentences might just string themselves along in such a fashion as to reflect the style of that great Australian all-rounder.

A Contemporary Issue

Many of the ideas and experiences discussed in this book will relate to issues that people have faced since time itself was born. In contrast, some of the ideas may seem to belong specifically to the last decade of the twentieth century, and I am not ashamed of that. This is inescapable, since my ideas and opinions have been forged within the context of recent medical practices and social trends. Nevertheless, I can claim – rather smugly – that forward planning is one of my strengths, and I like to feel that there really are some rather progressive elements within this book. As the twenty-first century unfolds, a little progression, at least, is an absolute necessity. I dare, even, to suggest that the following pages will reveal a forward momentum that has been inspired first by the expectancy, and now by the arrival of the new Millennium.

PART 1

A Conception of Happiness

1

INITIAL CONSIDERATIONS

There are many different aspects to consider before planning a baby.

Financial Concerns

There is the obvious question of expense – a 64,000-dollar question if ever there was one. At some stage, you are bound to ask yourself 'Can we afford to bring up a child?' A variation on the theme might be 'Can we afford to bring up a child and maintain our current lifestyle?' A further variation might be 'Well, we can afford a child now, but what will happen if our circumstances change, and how will we provide for our offspring later in life?' Having to cope with the unexpected is always a risk. Even if the outgoings connected with one little dependant can easily be covered, will the sums still add up if the affordable single baby turns out to be twins? All these questions weigh heavily on the mind.

We would all like to feel that money is not the dominant factor in our lives, but it would be extremely unwise to discount the importance of financial matters absolutely. Society constantly finds new ways of placing demands on the parental pocket. There is only one viable response. People dig and delve ever deeper in order to meet those demands. Life must go on, even if it costs, in monetary terms, more than we would ideally like to pay. Happy are those who really do know that money is not the true issue.

I like to believe that I have a realistically optimistic outlook on life. Whilst I acknowledge the potential difficulties, I also recognize the potential opportunities. My gut reaction to the question of affordability is to say 'Somehow we will manage.' For some people, simply managing is not enough, and this may be the key factor in deciding to delay, or even to resist altogether the beginning of a family. It is not for me to criticize other people's views and decisions. I would simply say that I would consider myself selfish in the extreme if I were to value an affluent, childless lifestyle above a financially difficult but loving family lifestyle. I do stress, here, that this is merely a personal view. I do not, for one minute, expect that everyone will share my code of values. Life would be frightfully dull if that were the case.

Assuming, though, that you have decided to have children, the next important question will be how many children to have. Again, financial circumstances play a key role here. You keep coming back to the realization that the more children you have, the more you will have to pay out in expenses for food, clothing, holidays, and education, education, education (thanks to Tony Blair for that last phrase). Then there is further education. Does it ever end? The expense is not always based on a simple multiplication of each individual cost by the number of children, but, generally speaking, each extra child will add significantly to the overall drain on resources.

Logistics

In addition to the question of affordability, there is also the crucial issue of logistics. Conventional car designs, for example, allow for four passengers: two adults and two children. It is as if the manufacturers of both cars and children's car seats have collaborated in order to determine the pattern of family life. Having more than two young children to transport will prove extremely difficult, unless you are in the fortunate possession of a so-called multipurpose vehicle. The ownership of MPVs could take us back again to the question of financial resources, but there are other avenues to explore.

Car seats are, of course, an obvious example of the many aspects of life that affect family planning. Package holidays, also, tend to be geared towards families with two parents and two children. Modern housing styles are the most telling sign of all. The generally recognized standard includes three bedrooms; one for each of the independent little beings, and one for their conception.

Regeneration

On top of all these practical considerations, there is also a huge range of emotional issues to consider.

The first thing to emphasize here is that by deciding to have a family, you are committing to putting other people first, and to putting yourself out. To a certain degree, this commitment applies to financial matters and to material goods, but it applies even more to the emotions.

In many ways, having children is about sacrificing your own life, or at least certain aspects of it. Parents soon realize that the children they bring into the world are far more important than they, themselves, will ever be again. The outside world may not come to the same conclusion. The external appraisal of the different generations within a family is usually based on personality, wealth, career success, and impact on the world. What matters within the family is that the needs, desires, and ambitions of your offspring take precedence over your own. For parents, your children are your very own members of the next generation; a generation that will drive forward the whole process of life. In time, these children will be inspired by similar feelings relating to their own children. Without this commitment to regeneration, the reproductive process seems hollow and perfunctory.

In the great scheme of things, parental sacrifice is a

relatively minor consideration. Yes, your lifestyle will change. If it does not, there is something seriously wrong. Yes, your tolerance level will be stretched to the limit, and beyond. If this is not the case, you can expect to be accorded the rank and privileges of a saint. Yes, the whole scenario will be inconvenient. But, if life is easy, it will scarcely be rewarding. Whoever said that life was meant to be straightforward?

The State of the World

Having dismissed the potential deterrents of money difficulties, emotional challenges, and the inconvenience factor, there is still at least one more major hurdle to surmount. Many people have serious concerns about bringing children into the incredibly dangerous world in which we all live. I will acknowledge from the outset that I do not have a comforting answer to this problem.

Long before I was in a position to start a family, I was very much against the idea of being responsible for the introduction of another being to the cruelties of the age. I remember being frightened on behalf of children who, at that stage, were light years away from conception. It is difficult to assess the extent of all the evils that have such a detrimental effect on this world. It is perhaps more meaningful to talk in terms of threats, or potential evils. Those that stand out the most include car accidents, assault, murder, terrorism, war, and, arguably the biggest evil of all time, the threat of nuclear destruction.

Humanity is also threatened, though less deliberately, by increasing damage to the environment. Dwindling natural resources, pollution, global warming and corruption of the food chain all contribute to what could be considered, at best, as a less than satisfactory scenario, and, at worst, as a catastrophic series of global events. The world really can seem like a terrible place.

On top of the risk of introducing your offspring to all of

6

these physical menaces, there is also the area of mental and emotional hardship. People suffer in so many ways. Extreme cases may be caused by break-ups in relationships, long-term unemployment, or a general sense of being a failure in life. Moreover, there seems no limit to the extent to which people are prepared to be unkind to each other. Life is hard. If further proof of this is necessary, consider the number of people who are trying to buy out of their lives each week, by purchasing a ticket for the National Lottery.

With all this in mind, it almost seems hard to justify the continuation of the human race. I will not try to minimize the risks here. I simply reflect upon the fact that the world has always been hostile. Who are we to judge that now is the time to give up? Who are we to deny the next generations the chance to enjoy life, however difficult it may prove to be?

Taking the Plunge

Having given due consideration to all the concerns discussed above, the common reaction of potential parents is still to say 'What the heck' and 'We'll manage somehow'. Whilst this might sound a very flippant reaction to a very serious matter, it also offers an insight into the incredibly powerful life force that exists within the human spirit. Despite any number of possible disadvantages, the basic process of reproduction prevails. Humankind simply cannot be suppressed.

Drawing on intuition based on experience, my own personal view on life is that *things will work out*.

2

DAD'S THE WORD

To my mind, there are two ways of looking at the issue of telling others that you are having a go at adding to the population.

The Sensitive Approach

Telling a few selected loved ones that you are trying to start a family can be helpful in what is likely to be a highly emotive time. By revealing what is on your heart, you will be encouraging a deeper level of intimacy and will be paving the way for greater bonding with the people you choose to inform.

Unless you are extremely callous, trying to impregnate your wife will be a highly sensitive subject, and one that will dominate the mind. Should you manage to hit the jackpot with the first go, such preoccupation will be short-lived. In the more likely event that a result is not immediately forthcoming, a certain amount of tension may arise. As each month goes by without success, the self-imposed pressure will mount, and the task will become frustrating. Under these trying circumstances, it can help to have a confidant(e), or confidant(e)s, to help you through the difficulties. Be selective, though. Knowing that other people are expecting news adds to the pressure, so it is important not to share your confidence around too much. There is always the possibility, of course, that your plans may never come to fruition. Should this be the case, it may seem nobody can offer any real consolation.

Public Knowledge

On a much baser level, announcing that you are trying for a baby is equivalent to telling people that you are currently having sex, and lots of it. By providing more details, relating to schedules and the optimum time for conception, there is a serious risk of making the whole business sound like something out of *Only Fools and Horses* – the scenes where Rodney Plonker has to drop everything in order to comply with Cassandra's time chart are quite hilarious. I do not suggest that everybody will make this comparison, but bear in mind that being too open about such matters can make you end up looking a trifle foolish.

Jumping the Gun

However you decide to broach the subject, I would strongly recommend avoiding one thing in particular: announcing the good news that you have decided to have a baby. This surely is a way of counting chickens before the eggs have been fertilized; before they have even been approached by the sperms, in fact. By all means indicate that you would like a family in the near future, or that you are currently trying, but do not be any more presumptuous than that.

On one occasion, I found myself congratulating a colleague on his apparent success. I stopped, mid-sentence, on realizing that there was really nothing yet to celebrate, apart from the fact that he had renounced his child-free days and joined the ranks of those who consider children to be worth having.

A cocksure approach can often lead to egg on the face.

How embarrassing it would be to discover that, after months of bragging about having the most potent sperm gun in the world, it turns out that your Magnum has been firing blanks all along.

3

HOPES AND BELIEFS

In the opening chapter, I dealt with worries and concerns on a general or global level, in the context of debating the possibility of letting the sperm have a crack at the egg. Now, once fertilization has been well and truly accomplished, it is time to turn to some of the more personal issues that affect people who are shortly to become parents.

Blue or Pink?

Usually, the first area of speculation involves the sex of the unborn child. This used to be one of the most wonderful secrets that would only be divulged at the moment of delivery. Nowadays, it seems to be becoming increasingly popular for the sex to be known well in advance of the birth, with the help of ultrasound technology. In my case, I did not really want to know in advance. I cannot say that I did not try to look on-screen, but on both occasions I was fortunately unable to discern the telltale parts of the anatomy. I suspect that the radiographer could have made it easier, but chose not to. Some hospitals have a policy of deliberately not revealing the sex of the unborn child, for all sorts of commendable reasons.

There are, of course, other less technological ways of predicting, if not determining the sex. Clues can be found in the following: the nature of the morning sickness, the amount of kicking, and the shape of the pregnant mother's bulge. Based on how I had described all these features, a friend confidently predicted that our second child would be a boy, and her prediction subsequently turned out to be correct. On more of a medical note, it is said that some midwives can tell the sex by analyzing the pattern of the unborn baby's heartbeat. Clever people.

Contrasting Appeals

Apart from the interest generated by this guessing game, you have to question why the sex of the baby really matters. There may be all sorts of personal and cultural reasons for wanting either a girl or a boy. In my case, I had no real preference first time round, and only a slight preference the second time around. Various questions came to mind, including:

1) Did I want a boy so that the family name could be continued in traditional fashion?
2) Would I give the same welcome to a girl as I would to a boy?
3) Would I expect to bond more with a boy?
4) If a girl, would she ever want to accompany me to a test match?
5) Would a boy or a girl cause more trouble?

I arrived at the following answers:

1) no
2) yes
3) not really
4) probably
5) both – at different stages in their lives.

Suitable Attire

As for the conventional colours associated with boys and girls, I am convinced that there is nothing wrong with 'blue for a boy and pink for a girl'. In an age where the term 'politically correct' crops up in all sorts of inappropriate contexts, I prefer to maintain the traditional values associated with the dressing of babies.

When it comes to buying presents for new-born babies, I tend to choose outfits according to this scheme, so that even babies that are born into the most trendy and relaxed of families have at least one stereotypical garment that they can wear comfortably and without fear of being wrongly identified by passers-by. Without such helpful marks of distinction, baby boys with pretty faces and cute curls can easily look like baby girls. Cherubic features tend to be seen as feminine attributes, even though they are not exclusive to female infants. A few colour-coded clues can do wonders in helping identify the specific type of creation on display, thereby preventing any awkward moments. At this stage, of course, babies themselves have neither the ability nor the inclination to deliberately deceive people about their sex. As for mischievous parents, wishing to rebel against sensible traditions, that is quite another matter.

From Pale Face to Exotic Countenance

Rather than wondering a great deal about whether our first child would be a boy or a girl, I was far more interested to see what colour he or she would turn out to be. Given Nature's capacity to blend all sorts of ancestral genes in any possible combination, there was potential for our baby to be any one of several different colours. The leading contenders were white, black, and something in between. Funny how a mixture of white and black never comes out grey.

When baby was born, I could not help but notice that her

colouring was closer to her father's than her mother's, and this was a very minor disappointment to me. Still, children rarely retain the colour they present at birth. Since that wonderful occasion, Georgina's colour scheme has indeed altered considerably, and she now looks very much more like a mixture. I would say a 'dolly mixture', but that would scarcely do her justice. Suffice to say that Georgina is a real sweetie, and even more adorable in that she now displays more of her mother's charms.

If 'dolly mixture' is not a very suitable term to use, then I think that 'Dolly Dealer' might just be marginally more appropriate. But only just. If we were to ask one hundred fathers 'Would they allow their daughter to appear in a shimmering, figure-hugging frock on a Friday night game show?' the number that said 'Yes' would probably be lower rather than higher. Personally, I would not mind one little bit, and if Bruce Forsyth is still playing his cards right in about sixteen years' time, Georgina could well become the most appealing dolly ever to do her dealing. Still, I am digressing here. Comparing innocent babies with television babes is like comparing apples with pears. And, as we all know, you get nothing for a pear; not in this game.

The Developing Being

If you will allow me to temporarily interrupt the current time and space continuum, let us briefly look forward a little. A year to the day on which a baby is born, the first birthday will be celebrated. This will be, of course, a significant landmark for all concerned, and one that should never be allowed to pass by unnoticed. A light sponge cake, with jam and cream in the middle, soft white icing, and a single, prominent candle in the centre is my favourite way of marking the event; on baby's behalf, of course.

Despite the pleasure derived from a birthday, I cannot help but feel that we all get the timing of the celebration hugely wrong. To my mind, the baby's life really starts at conception, and hence the age should be measured from this point. Granted, there is some degree of vagueness here, but this rather adds a certain charm to the occasion. In a world that strives to attain ever-increasing levels of scientific precision and control, I find it pleasantly ironic that we will never know, for sure, exactly when we first came into existence.

I do not imagine that this viewpoint will be universally attractive. Still, nothing will shake me from the belief that by the time of its first official birthday, a baby will actually be one year and nine months old, give or take a few days.

4

FEARS, CONFIDENCE, AND PERSPECTIVE

Fears To Be Conquered

Unless you are the complete optimist, with no worries whatsoever in life, you will probably experience a variety of fears during pregnancy. These fears may range from minor niggles to major concerns. They may linger in the mind for just a few seconds, or they may have a rather more lasting effect. If dwelt upon, the fears can assume awesome proportions, and may have a seriously detrimental effect on the emotional well-being of the expectant parent. Obviously, the extent of each fear will be governed by the individual personality.

Ten possible fears – in roughly chronological order:

1) The initial fear, in attempting to procreate, of being unable to have children. Infertility is always a possibility, and one which is apparently increasing all the time. Sperm counts are dropping, due largely to the effects of the environment on the male reproductive capabilities.
2) Having crossed the first bridge, there is now a fear of the baby not surviving during the term of pregnancy. Pregnancies may be ectopic, or they may result in miscarriages. In other cases, babies may simply not

be strong enough to survive the full duration, and will thus be stillborn.

3) The fear of injury to the mother, and thus to the unborn child. This might occur in road traffic accidents, or in cases of assault, or in any number of other dangerous scenarios.

4) The father's fear of dying before the arrival of the child. Especially, again, the fear of dying in a car accident, which somehow seems particularly horrific.

5) The fear of going blind before ever seeing the new baby. Perhaps the least likely of all the possible contingencies listed here, and perhaps the most irrational, but it still might cross the mind.

6) The fear of causing the baby distress by not knowing how to handle it. Failing to support the baby's head could result in serious neck injuries. Unlikely, but possible. Dropping the baby is also to be dreaded.

7) The fear of not responding to the charms of the baby. This might mean not being able to offer a loving welcome into the family. Taken to an extreme, it could result in outright rejection of the new-born child.

8) The fear that the baby is about to enter a cruel and distressing world.

9) Following on, during the baby's formative stages, there is a risk of cot death. Scientists have still not provided a definitive explanation for this terrible event.

10) Far less serious, but still potentially damaging, is the fear of not living up to the child's expectations in times to come. Alternatively, there might be a fear of not being able to provide for the little one, financially or otherwise.

This is not an exhaustive list, of course, and you will probably be able to add some of your own concerns.

*

Morbid and unpleasant thoughts these may be, but most of them will probably flash through your mind at least once during the pregnancy. Some may be just too improbable to occupy any time at all; others might threaten to become dominant. The important thing is to keep all concerns in perspective. Whilst I claim, elsewhere in this book, to practise cautious optimism, I tend to consider all imaginable eventualities. This arises out of compulsive curiosity, rather than from a deliberate wish to disturb myself. All things considered, I believe that this level of awareness brings more advantages than disadvantages.

In most cases, the fears will almost certainly be greater the first time round. Having a first baby is, of course, a new and daunting experience, full of all sorts of major challenges and difficulties. Once the first baby is down and dusted, confidence comes flooding back. Second pregnancies are generally much easier to handle. Then, of course, there is the danger of becoming complacent!

Amniocentesis

One fear that I did not include in the foregoing list is the fear of having a baby that is born handicapped. I feel that this issue deserves rather deeper consideration. An important aspect of this subject, and one that attracts some controversy (although in my view not enough controversy), is the practice of amniocentesis. Amniocentesis is the extraction of a sample of amniotic fluid for examination, as a means of assessing the unborn child's potential for developing a damaging medical condition. The option to undergo this test will be mentioned, and sometimes recommended, especially when the medical experts consider that there is an increased likelihood of a problem. Factors that affect this likelihood include the age of the mother and the genetic make-up of both parents. Should the tests reveal that something is wrong, termination of pregnancy is discussed.

To my mind there is a widespread acceptance that perfect

health is all-important. Neither Angela nor I wished to consider the possibility of having such a test. This was not because we were squeamish about needles, but because we were prepared to accept the baby under any circumstances. Having had two healthy babies, it may now seem very easy to hold this view. However, this genuinely was the view that we both took during the pregnancies. The point I am trying to put across is not that there is a right or a wrong way to feel, but that there are alternatives. People react and adapt to their own individual circumstances. Coming to terms with ill health is, regrettably, an important part of many people's lives. There is no standard way to go about it.

As Long as It's Healthy

Leading up to the birth of Georgina, our first child, I lost track of the number of people who said to me 'Would you prefer a girl or a boy? I suppose you don't mind, as long as it's healthy.' I imagine that nearly everyone has made this comment on at least one occasion, and I am sure that nobody ever means any harm in voicing this rather hackneyed opinion. If anything, it reveals a certain amount of interest and concern for the well-being of one's self and family. However, I do find the statement somewhat vexing, and I think the sentiments behind the opinion need challenging.

Of course, expectant parents hope to have a perfectly healthy child. It would be unnatural not to. My objection to this standard view is that it implies that an imperfect child (whatever that might mean) would not really be welcomed or valued by the parents. Without wishing to sound overly self-righteous, I do not share this view. I admit that in my own experience, fortune has smiled on me just about absolutely. It is no wonder, one might think, that I can be so positive about this subject.

Paradoxically, I believe that my opinions on this matter have been heavily influenced by the experience of being the uncle of a child with severe disabilities. My niece was perfectly healthy at birth, but her subsequent development has been retarded due to the ill effects of meningitis, which she contracted when still only a few days old. At first, I felt bemused. When the situation began to feel more real, I felt sad and disappointed. These feelings have never really gone away. However, my niece did not become any less dear to me after the illness began. If anything, I felt even more love for both my niece and for my sister. Here was a dream, a tiny baby, the first of her generation in our family, and all the more special because she required extra attention at such a tender young age.

Life has been hard. These words are too feeble to express the emotions that have been evoked, or to describe the challenges that have arisen in recent years. Deep down, I regret not spending more time with my niece in order to get to know her better. Even so, I have known her well enough to see how meaningful her life has been. This little girl, a star shining upon the lives of my sister and all her family and friends, has enriched the lives of many people. Throughout all the suffering, there has been joy.

I do not wish to sound simplistic here, or to suggest that there are some easy conclusions that can be drawn. There never are when it comes to matters that are so deeply personal. Still, for the reasons that I have related above, I would gently assert that it is not *all*-important for a baby to be perfectly healthy. This does not mean that I regard illness as an insignificant event or as some sort of potential blessing in disguise. Far from it. In serious cases, the suffering will be deep and long-lasting. I simply mean that good health, though preferable, is not necessarily the only important factor. Some things in life cannot be changed; they have to be experienced as they are.

Perspective on the Future

Expectant parents may normally be full of confidence and hope. Medicine has advanced enormously in our times, and serious problems tend to make the news because they are exceptions to the rule. Generally speaking, we tend to expect that bad luck will happen to someone else. Still, on occasions, at least, there will be cause to worry about the possibility of things going wrong. In some ways, it may be beneficial to have such thoughts, to prevent complacency from setting in. Being blind to the potential dangers prevents people from taking all the necessary caution in the events leading up to and during childbirth.

Of course, even if you are fully aware of all the risks, and take all possible measures to prepare for the safe arrival and the continued good health of a child, the ensuing events may be out of your control. From this point of view, fearing injury and death seems to be perfectly understandable. I would even say that it may help to envisage the worst-case scenario, as in many aspects of life.

However, the worst-case scenario will probably never arise. Until or unless it does, dwelling extensively on such thoughts is unhealthy. The negative should be placed in its proper perspective. There are so many positive factors to consider. As a general rule, having children is an incredibly joyful and refreshing experience. The sense of wonder surrounding the birth of a child is tremendous. The appearance of the baby's head is the culmination of a long and arduous ordeal, but it is also a triumph over all the difficulties and risks posed up until that point. The baby's first act of crying could be interpreted as an expression of suffering and pain on coming into the world. I prefer to regard it as a dramatically vocal negation of all the threats and dangers. The life force of a new-born child is both a physical and a symbolic testimony to the powerful continuity of humankind. The vivacious, innocent happiness of a developing child is simply one of the most wonderful stages in life.

We cannot completely control our lives, and we do not

know exactly how the future will unfold. We can, however, exert some influence by taking advantage of the opportunity to procreate. The blessings that our children bestow upon us are innumerable. Even when we do not feel so blessed, I do not believe that having children is something to regret. I know there are, and will always be tragedies that challenge this positive approach. The only conclusion I can reach is that there will always be at least some happiness arising out of the experience of having children, and in the vast majority of cases, a great deal of happiness.

5

COPING WITH PREGNANCY

Fat Controlling

One of the inescapable features of pregnancy is that the woman becomes fat. This might sound like an insult, but none is intended. Pregnant women are the first to admit that they are fat, and deserve credit for doing so, even if – as Basil Fawlty would say – they are merely stating the bloomin' obvious. In turn it would take a hugely respectful, courteous, and probably very dull man not to call his partner 'fat' on at least one occasion during the pregnancy. If not 'fat', then a similar comment will made in reference to the pregnant woman's changing shape. Not referring to this major change would indicate either a partial or total disinterest in the partner and the matter at hand.

The important issue here is not the use of particular language to describe a particular state of being, but the effect to which such comments are made, and the affection – or lack of it – behind them. In normal circumstances, references to another person's increasing size are not welcome, and may be deemed insulting. Within the context of pregnancy, drawing attention to size may well be grounded in affection, and in a genuine wish to add value to the relationship. At the very least, such attention should result in some light-hearted banter. Of course, there is always a time and a place for this kind of interplay. It is quite possible to pick precisely the wrong time and place, although well-intended comments will usually be received favourably.

23

For various reasons, a man may feel extremely pleased to see his partner becoming larger and larger. For starters, it will show him that the pregnancy really is happening. After the initial discovery, it can be several months before the woman actually starts to look pregnant. On a wider level, the increasing bulge will become more and more visible to other people, and will thus act as a kind of status symbol for both parties involved.

I have fond memories of an interchange with one of the locals whilst on holiday in Montego Bay, Jamaica. Having just walked out of Doctor's Cave Beach Club, I was making my way along the road with Angela, who at that point was about halfway through her term. As we passed by a group of young men, one of them boldly called out to me: 'That's a fine piece of work, sir, a fine piece of work.' It took me a moment to realize that he was speaking to me, and that he was referring to my wife's condition. On realization, I felt myself beaming with pride, and all I could do was smile back in his direction. A few days later, we walked along the same stretch of road, and this time we were accompanied by our delightful eighteen-month-old daughter. On seeing us again, the same young man called out 'A fi him Pickni.' Translated into straight English, this meant 'She belongs to him, no doubt about it.'

Looking back on these two very casual and minor interchanges, it is pleasant to reflect on the kind sentiments expressed and received. The man who, up until a few days previously, had been a complete stranger, had been kind enough to publicly express respect for the family concerns that were very close to my heart. First, he had acknowledged that I had been skilful in making my wife pregnant. Such admiration for my virility was not to be dismissed lightly. Secondly, he had pointed out the family resemblance between myself and my daughter. I am always delighted by such a comparison. Fortunately for Georgina, she has plenty of time to grow out of this somewhat unfortunate similarity. Babies have done nothing to deserve looking like their parents, and, as luck would have it, thankfully often manage to disinherit some of the bad parental features, to enhance still further some of the good ones, and eventually to end up being far better-looking than both mother and father. But, back to Montego Bay and the effects of the maximum respect displayed by a new-found friend. On two counts my ego received a tremendous boost. I sincerely hope that the pleasant young man took some reward of his own from the proud, amused reaction that must have been written all over my face. How impressionable the male ego is.

Leaving aside the male ego just for a moment (a fat chance of that, you may think), let us return to the main subject of this chapter: female increase, and the male appreciation thereof (*see what I mean?*).

Another reason for a man to be pleased with the state of increase in female flesh is that this change provides a constant reminder of the fragility of the little being inside the pregnant woman. The blubber, for want of a more scientific term, is necessary to protect and nourish the unborn child, and is therefore a vital agent within the process. The expression 'keeping the baby warm' is rather twee, but it does describe one of the essential functions being performed by the woman's developing body. The fragile being is dependent on the host not only for food and air, but also for a soft, comfortable, safe environment in which to grow. A fat tummy plays a key role in providing that all-important cushioning effect.

You can therefore marvel at the way that pregnant women selflessly put themselves at an indisposition, losing their shape in the process, in order to safeguard the growth of the little people inside them.

Craving

Craving is an important feature of the woman's diet during pregnancy. For the woman, satisfying these cravings can easily seem like a justifiable and reasonable course of action. As far as the man is concerned, a woman's cravings might seem inexplicable, and the need for satisfying them will not appear all that great. A sympathetic partner will, of course, endeavour to understand and to accommodate the craver whenever possible.

During both of Angela's pregnancies, I had to learn to appreciate the craving for the following simple food items: eggs and bacon, beanburgers, and raw oats. None of these are unusual in themselves, but they are not normally dishes that are consumed frequently in our household.

I suppose I should be grateful that I was not called upon to provide ice cream with pickled gherkins. This strikes me as being the most peculiar of combinations, and I rather fancy it to be a dish that is called for only out of a strange willingness to comply with the stereotypical image of the mad, craving, pregnant woman.

As far as I could see, Angela's body was undergoing a number of changes, one of which being a heightening in taste for a number of normally low-priority food items. The desire for a fried breakfast every morning could well have been a subconscious, angry reaction to the body's hormonal changes, manifesting itself in the form of a junk-food assault on the body itself. This could be stretching things a little. It could simply have been a change in tastes arising out of a changed set of circumstances. I do not claim to understand the science behind the craving for the given items. I am not sure, in fact, that science has all that much to do with it. Whether there is scientific import to this or not, it was a fact that my mother-in-law also had a craving for oats when she was expecting my wife.

However, should the food items in question be highly fatty and full of calories, giving into temptation excessively can lead to an undesired rate of increase in weight. As in all cases, diet is only one factor when it comes to determining the size and shape of the human body. Exercise is equally, if not more, important. During pregnancy, diet may assume greater importance, since normal and regular exercise may not always be possible.

Excessive Increase

As discussed above, there is great virtue, and no shame in losing your figure for the sake of a baby. It is possible, though, to allow the padding factor to be unnecessarily great. The unborn child requires only so much cushioning. There is also a limit to the size recommended for the pregnant woman. Putting on weight excessively is not only unnecessary for both woman and child, it also makes losing the weight all that much harder after the baby has been born.

The man, on his part, should recognize the need to suggest such delights as going for a stroll around Windsor Great Park and going for a dip in the Caribbean. Exercise should be entertaining; it should not be a drudgery. The nearly new man owes it to his partner to help take her mind off her immediate condition, and to open her eyes to the world continuing all around. Maintaining a proper level of exercise will also improve the chances of a smooth delivery. The alternative, i.e. sitting around as a couch potato, merely leads to difficulties all along.

Should excess become a possibility, despite all the positive male contributions described here, the man should take it upon himself to offer a few well-chosen opinions on the extent to which the woman's size should reach. It might not help all that much in a practical sense, but at least he will feel that *he* has performed his duty.

Male Weight Gain

It is always possible, of course, that the father may also put on weight during the course of the pregnancy. This could be regarded as sympathizing with the mother's plight to an unnecessary extreme. It could also result from an abnegation of sharing the various exercise routines. Laziness is also an outside possibility.

It is more likely that male weight gain will occur once the baby has been born. This may follow on from a temporary loss of weight, achieved during labour. Taking the starting point as the entry into the labour ward, our first child took the best part of a weekend to arrive. During this long and drawn-out delivery, I lost approximately one stone in weight. This was due not only to stress and concern, but more so to a lack of any easily available nourishment. Consequently, by the time I arrived home, some time after the birth, I was a thin shadow of my former self. Needless to say, it all came back again, with interest.

Having brought baby back home, the father's movements will be severely restricted. Even if you have the inclination, finding the time to go out and keep fit can be difficult. This may be the case because the mother has left father holding the baby, as she spends all her spare time trying to regain her own original figure. Still, this chapter is running on a bit too far ahead of itself. Time to let the issue sit down and rest for a while.

6

PARENTCRAFT

In preparation for the birth of your baby, you will normally be invited and probably expected to turn up for antenatal classes. The common term for these classes nowadays is 'Parentcraft'. One of the effects of this crafty term is to make the classes seem obligatory for both the mother-to-be and the father-to-be. In the past, antenatal classes would have been meant mainly for women, and would have been based around breathing exercises and other matters relating to delivery. Parentcraft classes, however, involve a whole range of issues that thoroughly involve the father just as much as the mother. At least, that's how the midwife likes to put things across.

In my case, I was initially reluctant to attend; not because I was not interested, but because the classes were arranged on the same evenings that I would normally be attending winter cricket nets. Fortunately, I did not have to choose between the two, as the original class was oversubscribed, and we were invited to attend a series of classes hastily arranged to take place on Thursdays, rather than Tuesdays.

Having said this, I was still not very keen to go along. I suppose I felt I already knew just about enough to get by. I also expected to find myself having to take part in a series of practical activities with cushions on the floor. At best, I thought I would find the classes a bit tedious. To my surprise, the classes took the form of seminars, presented by a very experienced, very open, and very amusing midwife. I was rather surprised to find myself fascinated by what she had to say. She managed to put across important scientific information in a humorous manner. Her anecdotes and digressions were funny, but not so hilarious that they took away from the gravity of the knowledge being imparted.

More than a little theatricality shone through in her demonstration of a doll's head navigating a course through a model of a woman's pelvis, to represent the difficulties a baby has in making its way out into the great, wide world. This provided a simple but effective means of showing one of the reasons why the mother can find herself in such discomfort during labour. Our midwife threw out the term 'bone on bone' to describe the close relationship between the baby's skull and the mother's pelvic frame during the descent. It really is a tight squeeze!

In addition to the learning process, parentcraft classes help you to realize that you are not the only ones to be preparing for the big event. By being present in a room full of expectant mothers and fathers, you realize that you are not unique. It is sometimes important to be brought down to earth in this fashion. Whilst preparing to become parents may currently be the most important aspect of your lives, you yourselves are not the centre of the universe.

The downside to these classes is that the men, as well as the women, do have to do breathing exercises after all, although in our case, not on the floor.

7

THE NAMING CONVENTION

Legally, after the baby has been born, you have six weeks to register the birth, and thus the names of your new-born offspring. Six weeks is, of course, rather a long time to make a baby wait for a name, even if the delay affects friends and family more than the baby itself. You may well take just a few days, or perhaps just a few minutes to come up with the name. In many cases, parents-to-be have their names sorted out well in advance of the birth.

The naming process can provide hours of fun or frustration, or perhaps even a combination of the two. It may well be wise not to lay all your cards on the table to begin with. You will need at least one ace to bring out from your sleeve after your partner has dismissed a series of opening suggestions.

There are so many factors to consider, not least the number of names. Famous cricketers tend to have three initials before the surname – I.V.A. Richards and P.C.R. Tufnell to name but two – so three it had to be for us. Other lesser considerations include how the first name might be shortened (or lengthened) into nicknames, any potential acronyms made up by the initials, family connections, and the choice between originality and traditionalism. Think carefully; your child may grow up to despise an outlandish name, or, equally, to rue the fact that there are four others in the class who share the same unadventurous name.

Here are two examples of the difficulties in coming to an agreement with your partner on names. I have always liked the name Lois. Unluckily for me, my wife could only associate the name with Lois Lane, Superman's reporter girlfriend. Well, having watched, together, every episode of *The New Adventures of Superman*, and never having come across another Lois in any other walk of life, that may well have been a valid objection. I don't think my wife was too keen to be reminded of Teri Hatcher (recently voted as 'most wanted female' in *For Him Magazine*) every time the baby's name was spoken. Still, we later frequently called our baby 'Superbabe', which, in different ways, is reminiscent of both the Lois and Clark characters.

My wife's initial favourite was Jemima. Now, it seemed to me that the name Jemima was more than a match for Lois in terms of waddling out of a work of fiction and onto our respective shortlists. Whilst conceding that Thomas Hardy's mother, and probably a good many other notable figures in history, was called Jemima, who could argue with the fact that the name is inextricably linked with the surname Puddleduck? Beatrix Potter's creation could stay well and truly on the page, as far as I was concerned. There was the equalizer. In the end, the baby turned out to be a boy, so we needn't have troubled ourselves with these two controversial options after all.

Some friends of ours took a seemingly interminable four weeks to inform officialdom of their latest creation. Our card of congratulations had to refer, in Clint Eastwood fashion, to the 'baby with no name'. After two weeks, our friends misled us with a shortlist of probable possibilities, including Sarah, Victoria, and Josephine. In the end, they named their little girl after a popular variety of potato. On a recent visit, I couldn't help myself from gazing into her deep brown eyes, and then referring to her as 'Spud-U-Like'. Perhaps not everyone links the name Desiree to a potato; perhaps it's just my warped sense of humour. Still, I hope her parents don't develop a chip on their shoulders.

8

PREPARING THE HOME

It is amazing how much drive a pregnant woman can have in the last few weeks of her term. Maybe the energy is born out of a sense of frustration at having been weighed down all this time by the bulge in front of her. The last quarter of the term tends to feel the longest, and even though the end is getting closer and closer, the whole thing seems to drag on and on. Hence, there is a need to channel this pent-up energy into some meaningful form of physical activity. Exercise can come into play here, although this in itself is not sufficient. There is an overriding will to take part in something creative and lasting.

Pregnancy can bring with it a host of niggling aches and pains, and sometimes more serious disorders that can cause the woman to be either unable or unwilling to exert herself. Early on, it may simply have been a case of not having had the lift. Now, however, with the finishing line in sight, the lift suddenly comes back. Both mother-to-be and father-to-be will feel able to tackle almost any DIY task with a renewed sense of vigour.

One very useful activity is decorating. Unless you live in an already perfect house, with every room decorated just as you like it, there will usually be something to attend to. In many cases, the nursery may still be unprepared well into the last quarter. Often, the intention will have been to have done this earlier in the term, but circumstances will not have allowed it. At this stage, given the possibility of baby arriving before the due date, you can never rely on being able to complete the job in time. Still, unless there are any strong indications otherwise, you can reasonably expect that there will be time to do something. Being told by people 'It could be any time, now' can be irksome, since those last few weeks are so important for getting things done.

Having long ago watched Angela perform the lioness's share of the work in laying down loft insulation, I was fully aware of her capabilities in the field of home improvements. Now, I was even more impressed by the sight of her halfway up a ladder, holding a piece of wallpaper in one hand and a brush in the other, and all this with less than four weeks to go before the due date. The fact that I was playing the role of lackey to her master craftswoman was not really that startling, but the image of a hugely pregnant woman in this kind of action really was quite special. As a bonus, the wall ended up looking quite beautiful. Even more impressively, this was not an isolated piece of action. Having made a fine job of the nursery, Angela then went on to mastermind the repapering of the living room. I take my cowboy hat off to her.

Inspired by this performance, I suddenly found myself branching out on my own. My major contribution to the renovations involved removing all the tiles from the walls in the bathroom. Having begun by poking around, just to see if one specific tile was loose, the desire to continue was just too great. Sending hundreds of ceramic tiles clattering to the floor was great fun, although it did rather leave the bathroom looking a bit grey and ugly. As a result, Angela decided that it would be nice to totally replace the old pink bathroom suite with a pristine, new white suite, set within a fully re-tiled room, in preparation for all the baths that our imminent baby would shortly be taking. The idea of a baby splashing around in a grey and grotty bathroom was quite unacceptable. At this point, it was time to call in a professional builder. There is, after all, a limit to one's energy reserves.

Buying for Baby

Whilst preparing a nursery, it will have crossed your mind to consider the purchase of a selection of a few key items, including a Moses basket, a cot, a carrycot, a musical mobile, a pram, a pushchair, a high chair, a rocking chair ... did I say a few items? Not all of these will be needed immediately after the birth, of course, but they will probably all be recommended by overeager sales assistants. With luck, you may receive hand-me-downs from family and friends who no longer plan to have any more babies. If not, it will be time to go and have a browse at what there is on offer from the likes of Mamas and Papas, Cosatto, Maclaren, and Silver Cross.

Pasta Masters

Nowadays, the choice on offer is staggering. One thing that will stand out is that the Italians fancy themselves as a nation of baby-lovers. The range of Italian-produced baby goods is enormous. Moreover, they do it all with such elegance. The fabrics and the designs would not be out of place on a Milanese catwalk. The gadgets, the solidity, the sleekness, and the versatility of the equipment must owe something to the Italian car industry. Everything, in fact, looks incredibly stylish.

From the huge range available, we settled on a Mamas and Papas 'Baby Chic': a three-in-one cross between pram, carrycot, and pushchair. With swivel wheels, of course. The price? Well, several hundreds of pounds; but then, baby is worth it. The very latest model, I gather, is an all-terrain three-wheeler. Sounds more like a cross between a Land Rover Discovery and a Reliant Robin than the height of fashion for a baby looking for a slick set of wheels. Sounds like more money, too.

9

THE PLEASURE PRINCIPLE

Whilst sex is probably inadvisable during the early stages, it can be indulged in fairly comfortably mid-term, and is positively recommended by midwives late on, especially as the due date approaches with no sign of the baby coming out of its own accord.

Having sex during pregnancy can, I am reliably informed, be an immensely exciting experience. This may well be for a number of reasons. I merely speculate, but the following may offer some explanation as to why pregnancy should heighten the enjoyment:

☺ During this time, sex feels even more mischievous than usual.

☺ It is also likely to be in short supply, so when it happens, it feels all the more intense.

☺ It can be fun to re-enact the cherished night of passion that resulted in the present situation.

☺ Sex is something you do not *need* to do any more to prove that you are a man. Relax! Conception was achieved some time ago, so just enjoy the moment.

☺ Finally, changing hormones can have all sorts of effects on a woman's body, and this increase in potential excitement is just one of those changes.

I do not intend to dwell on this subject. Since it is a highly personal affair, I offer no relevant examples from my own experience. Suffice to conclude that it is possible, it is permissible, and it can be pleasurable.

PART 2

The Delivery

10

POSSIBILITIES AND ALTERNATIVES

Engaging

In the weeks and months leading up to the expected date of arrival, babies are prone to move around and position themselves in all sorts of ways.

Whilst I hesitate to use the term 'normal' when it comes to pregnancy and childbirth, babies normally begin to lower themselves about two weeks before they are likely to be born. This is generally the case with first babies. In the case of subsequent babies, engagement might not take place until shortly before the onset of labour. One thing that is for certain, friends and family will always ask the question 'Is the baby engaged yet?' Some will also offer an opinion as to high the baby is being carried. The term 'carrying low' implies, of course, that labour is not very far away.

The last few weeks can seem like forever, and it became clear to us that our baby did not wish to lower herself into the prescribed position within the expected time-frame. In hindsight, this can be seen as Georgina setting an early precedent for establishing her own schedules. Simply talking to her did not seem to have any effect. Even commanding her to engage, in a manner that Jean-Luc Picard (of the *USS Enterprise*) would have been proud of, did not do the trick. Eventually, the procrastination came to an end, as engagement took place around about the due date. However, engagement is not the same as total commitment. In most cases, there is still time for further reflection before the baby finally knocks on the door of the oven and asks to come out, just as the Gingerbread Man did. In our case, nine more days were to elapse, with precious few signs of any further activity, before induction was finally commenced.

Induction

Induction is meant to be a simple process. Basically, it entails giving a baby an ultimatum: 'Come out now, or the knife will be sharpened.' Nobody likes to feel rushed, and who could blame a baby for wanting to remain within the warm and cosy host environment. But, out it must come, and far better to be induced than to have to recite 'Is this a scalpel I see before me?' on the way to the theatre.

Parents-to-be have a right, of course, to hesitate. If you really are against the idea of induction, let the consultant know. It may buy just a little more time to allow a more spontaneous outcome. There is, of course, a danger of overcooking, and you will have to be aware of all the implications therein. Mr. Tarka, the consultant called upon to assess the overdue state of the pregnancy, understood our reluctance to induce, but politely pointed out that he would not dream of telling us how to do our jobs, and in return, did not expect us to tell him how to do his. Mr. Tarka put this across in such a charming manner that we couldn't help but be impressed by his opinions.

Despite agreeing with this professional advice, we still did not feel happy about an induction. We decided to hold out for just a few more days, and tried to put the idea of Wexham Park Hospital out of our minds by playing golf at the local pitch-and-putt course. Well, I was playing, and Angela was walking round, caddying for me. Boy, those clubs must have been heavy; and all those lost balls that had to be retrieved! It was no wonder that there was puffing and panting on a grand scale. Later that evening, we were both surprised to be told by our respective mothers that it would be best to follow the consultant's advice. Feeling

42

increasingly uncomfortable about waiting and hoping, we decided to go to the hospital immediately.

In Control?

In retrospect, it turned out that going for an induction must have been the right decision, since Georgina was born with very long fingernails. This indicated that the due date extrapolated from the ultrasound scan measurements was, in fact, accurate, and that our baby had been ready to come out for some time. From this experience, I can now see that however much you want to retain personal control over events, it is also important to recognize good advice when it comes along, and even more important to act upon it.

It is easy to believe that by submitting to an induction, you are handing over control of the pregnancy to a medical team, and not allowing events to unfold naturally. I have two simple observations to make here:

1) Nature can be cruel. A natural unfolding of events does not always bring happiness to humans.
2) One of the potential benefits of induction is that it allows the mother to know that the baby is finally on the way. Non-induced labours involve a greater element of surprise. In this sense, induction hands over to the mother a certain degree of control.

An Interesting Turn of Events

Our second baby, Devon, elected to follow a similar time-scale, although in his case, the lack of engagement was accompanied by copious shifting, twisting and turning, right up until the last few days. Approximately three weeks before the due date, the baby was seen to be lying in 'landscape' fashion, i.e. horizontally across the womb. This position was far from satisfactory, in that if labour were to

43

begin under those circumstances, the baby would be compromised and an emergency section would probably be necessary.

This option was not very appealing, although, to us, it did not at the time seem very likely. Babies do, in many cases, move around right up until the end. Besides, Christmas was only two days away, and we weren't prepared for the event to happen so soon. Thankfully, on the first Monday after Christmas, an ultrasound scan showed that the baby was now in the correct 'portrait' position. This was fine up until a week later, when a further scan showed that the baby had reverted to its horizontal position. Once again, the possibility of a section was discussed. Finally, when it came round to the pre-induction consultation, the cephalic (head-down) position had been assumed once again, but this was not enough to prevent a second induction. Somehow or other, this was the second baby that had managed to head off in slightly the wrong direction.

The conclusion we chose to draw was that both our babies must have been so happy and comfortable within the womb that they simply did not wish to come out, and hence positioned themselves in such a way as to extend the gestation period as long as possible.

So much for induction. The second major alternative to the spontaneous delivery is potentially even more challenging, and one that people tend to get far more cut up about. This is, of course, the way that Julius, the one-time mighty leader of the Roman Empire, came to be delivered into the world.

The Caesarean

An Incisive Use of Language

Before I came to experience the whole baby process, I always understood that cutting open a woman's tummy to help the baby out, and to allow baby to bypass the potentially distressing rite of passage down the birth canal, was referred to as a Caesarean. This term is still commonly used, by both medical and non-medical people alike. However, the even more common term for this type of delivery is the 'section'. It sounds altogether more clinical, more specific in what it describes, possibly less worrying, and certainly less Roman. The term you use does not really matter, I suppose. The point I'm trying to make here is that as you get deeper into the scheme of things, you come across unexpected terms and expressions that make you think you are becoming initiated. Instead of using the standard language of the ordinary human, you begin to pick up the *lingua franca* of medicine, and that helps you to feel that you are more in control of the events that are dominating your life. This gives comfort in an area that may well seem to be otherwise frighteningly undesirable.

The Choice of Cut

Caesarean sections fall into two main categories: the planned and the emergency. A third category involves some combination of the two, where the operation is planned to start with, but ends up becoming an emergency.

Scheduled Sections

The planned section is similar in some ways to the idea of an induction. In both cases, there is an attempt to control the birth process. Both options involve the application of a helping hand to expedite the delivery. Again, in both cases, the safety of the mother and the child is also a key factor in deciding whether or not to use medical intervention.

On one level, having a section might be regarded as the best way to reduce, if not eradicate the pain associated with normal deliveries. If pain could be done away with in this fashion, then the majority of mothers-to-be might well insist on such a method of delivery every time. Pain, however, can never be totally avoided. Having a section may seem like the easy option when it comes to removing the baby from the womb, but there will be significant soreness to come. Whilst the operation is usually fairly straightforward, there is more to it than a quick slit, rumble around, and stitching up. As in all cases of major surgery, healing needs to take place. Whilst the end result of healing is comfort, the healing process can be quite painful.

Sections are also planned in order to reduce the potential dangers associated with difficult pregnancies. Unfavourable circumstances will not always lead to surgery, but consultants nowadays seem to be increasingly keen to use the Caesarean as a means of lowering the risks.

Desperate Remedies

The emergency section also involves an attempt to negate danger and to establish control, but within the highly pressurized time frame associated with all forms of emergency surgery. In this context, the concept of parental control flies out of the window, and it is left to the surgeon to establish a safe and stable situation.

During the operation, the father will be kept out of the operating theatre and left to wonder how mother and child are faring within. All hopes and dreams of witnessing the miracle of birth will be dashed by the absolute need for minimal distractions around the operating table. From this point of view, the episode will be harder for the father than the mother. The mother will probably be under a general anaesthetic, but the father will be fully conscious of, and challenged by the traumatic events.

Given that planned sections can become emergencies, the idea of 'sections on demand' will probably never really take off.

The *Star Trek* Alternative to Labour

Anyone who has followed the remarkable career of the holographic doctor on board *Voyager* will know that science fiction can tantalize us with some brilliant make-believe alternatives. One such alternative is the choice of bypassing

46

the normal labour process, and having the baby transported out of the womb. In one episode, Naomi Wildman, a half-human, half-alien baby was indeed delivered by this method. Within this highly technical operation, there was simply no need to wait for the cervix to dilate, nor for the mother to do any panting and groaning, nor even for any slicing of the abdomen. Rather than issuing the conventional command 'Push', or calling for the scalpel, the doctor simply asked his assistant to 'energize'. A few seconds later, after the baby's molecular structure had been disassembled into millions of fragments and then reassembled, the baby arrived outside of the womb, and began a life of Trekking. Now, that's what I call a pretty remarkable *out-of-body* experience.

11

THE BIG DAY

As in all matters, different people react in different ways to the realization that it's time for the main event to begin. Most deliveries nowadays are carried out in hospitals, and the journey to the delivery point – hopefully the hospital of your choice – can be full of adventure. It will probably be an experience that has been long-awaited, well-rehearsed, and regarded as a defining moment within the early stages of labour. For some, this journey is like a pilgrimage. For others, it might seem rather more like an inconvenience.

Despite any amount of careful planning, it is highly likely that the big moment will occur at a most unexpected time, and in most unhelpful circumstances. My sister-in-law has a funny tale to tell about how her partner rushed home from work in order to take her to hospital, only to fall down the stairs in all the excitement, and to require medical assistance for himself. In another case, a friend fondly described to me how one of her twins was already 'halfway out' before she had even got into the car to go to hospital.

My favourite story relating to the inconvenience factor was told to me during a discussion about baby matters over the course of a cricket tea. With some measure of mirth, and even a little admiration, my team-mate told me how, when the time came, his brother had refused to come up from the garage at the bottom of the garden. Apparently, an important league football match was due to be played that afternoon, and neither the pumping brother nor his bursting wife were going anywhere until all the balls had been inflated.

Father Attending the Birth

The current practice in this generation is for the father to be by the mother's bedside during labour. This seems normal now, but men have not always found themselves in this position, however caring they may have been in previous generations. My father was not present at my birth, and this was considered appropriate by all parties involved. As for me, I am grateful that Angela virtually took it for granted that I would be standing next to the delivery couch. Long before we entered the delivery ward, I had been presented with a tacit list of tasks to carry out on demand. These tasks included spraying Angela's face with Evian water, offering my hand to be squeezed during moments of discomfort, and simply being there to offer moral support. I was, of course, also required to remain awake – not as straightforward as it might sound.

However draining and distressing, the whole experience simply cries out to be shared. On one level, attending the birth will allow you to satisfy your scientific curiosity, with added interest generated through being personally involved. On a more emotional level, being there will give you the opportunity to experience an intensity of feeling that you have probably never reached before. The sensations involved may well never be surpassed; at least not until your second child is on the way out. In some ways, this focusing on the individual reactions to the event is ironic, in that procreation is all about sharing. Sharing, though, does not include going halves with your partner in bearing the physical pain; nor does it mean that you will both necessarily understand how each other is feeling. Paradoxically, being present at the birth not only encourages an incredible feeling of bonding with your partner, it also allows you access to a vast range of highly individual, unique emotional reactions.

In some cases, once the baby has been delivered, the mother may very quickly start to feel lonely, despite all the company around her. Having previously been the centre of attention – usually for many hours – there is the potential for her to be ignored in favour of the baby. Care should be taken to avoid this scenario. Fathers should remember at all times that their presence at the birth is not just to allow them to witness a magnificent spectacle. Involvement, whether active or passive, is essential in helping the mother to come through the ordeal as unscathed as possible. In Oscar terms, the father should strive to play the role of 'best supporting actor', although here, of course, the prize is infinitely superior to an Academy award.

12

LABOUR INTENSIVE

Pain during Induction

Throughout the lead-up to the labour period, the loving and caring male will almost certainly have been doing his utmost to make the mother as comfortable as possible. He will have tried his best to remove any pain that might have been disturbing his beloved. There comes a time, though, when the father will probably feel ambivalent towards the pain suffered by the mother. My experiences on both occasions were surprising to my wife, and apparently insensitive to a degree, but in my book highly rational and acceptable. The point is that having waited for so long – for nearly forty-two weeks in the case of our first – you really want to see a sign that something is happening.

During induction, it can seem like things are taking forever. The midwifery staff will begin by making it sound quite likely that one squirt of prostaglandin jelly will do the trick, and that labour could well be induced within a matter of hours. They will, of course, add that it quite often takes two squirts, and, in exceptional cases three. In very extreme cases, a prostaglandin drip can also be attached in the delivery room, to speed up the labour.

Well, after a number of hours during which nothing significant seems to have happened, you may well start to feel that the whole process could last for days, if not weeks, rather than hours. You will start to wonder whether you, as a partner who is required to be alert and supportive at all times, have the stamina to keep going throughout. You worry that you will be asleep when it finally happens, or that you will be so worn out by waiting that you will be unable to offer any real assistance or support to the person who is, after all, undergoing the ordeal.

So, when things finally start happening, or rather, when you finally start to recognize that things genuinely are progressing, then you will probably be excused for feeling relieved, if not pleased. To see your beloved in the pain of contractions, to see her nearly bending over in agony whilst taking a *stroll* round the wards (to try and get things going), is, of course, not a pleasant matter. It can be highly distressing. Still, it really does show that the baby is on its way. After waiting for so long, you really cannot be blamed too harshly for finally being able to discern the signs that the little one will shortly be emerging. Exactly how shortly is still a matter for conjecture, but at the very least, this has to be an improvement on just sitting and waiting and wondering. There is a limit to how many crosswords you can do before feeling the need to do something different. The first, and continuing signs of pain are obviously not the ideal difference that you would wish to see in these circumstances, but they are a very real and meaningful difference that cannot be waved away without at least some small measure of gratitude.

The best approach, for the caring partner, is probably to insist to his child-heavy and aching beloved that the pain is not the cause of male relief and satisfaction, it is merely a necessary, albeit highly regrettable phase that has to be undergone. You do not want pain to come because pain is normal, you simply want to see some light towards the end of the tunnel, and the pain is the only illumination available, however harsh.

Not Convinced?

As a postscript to this section, I should point out that Angela felt that it took a long time, and considerable bouts of pain, before I was convinced that things were on the move. I am not so sure that it took me all that long to realize. I think it is fairer to say that I did know that the pain was slowly building up, and that I was merely waiting for Angela to indicate when the pain was really meaningful. I had to stop myself from getting too excited too soon. Knowing that there was a long way to go, I did not wish to fool myself that events would suddenly race ahead.

In my defence, the midwifery staff also seemed to take a long time before deciding that the pain was really strong enough to require medicinal pain relief. They must have witnessed too many false alarms to get flustered by the comparatively gentle twinges occurring in the very early stages of labour.

Indignity

However cheerful an attitude the mother-to-be chooses to adopt, labour is full of indignities.

One of the more minor indignities involved in the process is the woman's need to pass water at the most inconvenient of times and in the most uncomfortable of settings. The function is awkward enough without having to request for a bedpan and then to perform the act in front of the midwife and partner who might both, for whatever reason, feel it necessary to remain in the room at this time. Still, there is always some humour to be had in these events. Angela and I both found it amusing when, in order to encourage a good wee, the midwife subtly turned on the tap at the basin and left it running, for no other apparent reason, until well after the necessary had been performed.

Internal / Vaginal Examinations

Probably the biggest of all indignities is having your nether regions regularly examined by a host of doctors and midwives. Remember the calving scenes in the programme *All Creatures Great and Small*? Well, midwives and doctors perform a similar act, by inserting a hand into the woman's orifice in much the same way as James Herriot used to insert his into the rear end of a cow. A quick rummage to check that everything is in the right position, a measurement of the cervix, and out again. Nowadays, gloves and jelly are applied to assist in the investigation of the lower innards of human females. I presume that modern-day vets do likewise with cows.

These internal examinations take place throughout labour. Apparently, each examination is a little more painful than the previous one. Pethidine or an epidural will negate any pain from this activity, but until the pain relief is taken, no amount of lubricant jelly can prevent the increasing level of soreness.

As a partner, you simply sit back and try to look away (I carried on reading my autobiography of Jack Russell, subtitled '*Unleashed*'). The scene is not pretty, and it is obvious that there is significant discomfort involved. From this point of view, you have to assume that the examiners, be they male or female, are totally unstimulated by what they are doing. It is all part of the job, and a far cry from anything recreational.

If, by chance, the examination reveals an increase in the dilation of the cervix, then the sticky rummaging and the fumbling does not seem a totally bad experience. Knowing that the magic ten-centimetre measurement is getting closer can be a real help.

In polite company, such examinations are probably not discussed at all. However, pregnancy and labour are not generally conducive to polite discussions, and the subject of examinations will probably crop up in conversation sooner or later. Whether you talk about internal examinations or vaginal examinations is, of course, a matter of discretion.

Private Matters

I have been suprised to note that women do not seem to be embarrassed about the predicament they find themselves in when giving birth. This applies during the build-up to labour, and to the labour period itself. What happens subsequently is another kettle of fish altogether. An examination by a GP, six weeks after the delivery, can be the cause of much embarrassment – especially if the GP happens to be a man. Presumably, the embarrassment here arises out of the fact that after six weeks things have returned to relative normality, whilst the delivery of the baby was performed within quite exceptional circumstances.

I would also expect new mothers to be more than a little bashful about talking to other people, particularly to men, about the intricacies of their recent spell in labour. This does not seem to be the case. Women seem more than happy to talk about the details to men; at least to those men whose partners have themselves gone through a similar experience.

The Breaking of the Waters

The breaking of the waters is a rather grand term for the puncturing of the membrane surrounding the amniotic fluid. It is an experience that many people will expect to happen spontaneously, as part of the onset of labour. Many believe that this is an event necessary to trigger off the labour. People will tell you stories of where they were when the moment happened. A close colleague at work gladly recalled, on more than one occasion, how she had been shopping in Boots when she suddenly began to feel as though she had wet herself. It was only when she got home that she realized the significance of the dampness. More generally speaking, it has been known for supermarkets to offer a year's supply of nappies to any woman whose waters break during a visit to one of their stores.

Surprisingly, perhaps, not all labours begin with such a moment of sudden unexpectedness. In fact, the membrane may remain intact until fairly late on in labour, and the real indication of the onset of labour is the beginning of the contractions.

In the case of our first baby, I felt somewhat cheated in that the waters never broke by themselves. In the course of the last few weeks of the term, I had gone to work each day hoping and expecting to be telephoned by my wife, to say that the waters had gone and could I please come home quickly in order to drive her to the hospital. When this scenario failed to materialize, I felt just a little deflated. In the end, the midwife had to use a plastic instrument with a hook to puncture the membrane, and even then there did not seem to be much fluid to come out. I had expected a torrent, and saw only a trickle. Still, never mind, it was not really such an important issue within the overall scheme.

The second time around, I was even more convinced that I would get the emergency telephone call. As the due date approached, with no real signs of an imminent cascade, we decided that a trip to the cinema might expedite matters. *Titanic* seemed appropriate, in that the vast quantity of water swirling all over the screen would surely provoke a similar gushing response from my wife. Still, it never came. However, this time, the midwife was not called upon to do the deed, as events eventually took a more natural course. Half an hour after entering the delivery suite, there was a brief moment of excitement, triggered by a sudden popping noise, similar to the sound that could be made by bursting a packet of crisps. This was followed up immediately by the forming of a pool of water on the delivery room floor. It may sound silly, but I was particularly proud of Angela at that moment, simply for providing that long-awaited moment of spontaneity.

At Her Worst?

Pre-pregnancy, a woman may be as slim as Naomi Campbell and as chic as Claudia Schiffer. During the pregnancy term, this comparison will lose most of its accuracy – both in terms of looks and deportment. Once inside the labour ward, elegance and grace will be but distant memories. Rather unfortunately, this metamorphosis is sometimes regarded as a basis for believing that a husband who attends the delivery of a baby will see his wife at her worst.

The following factors might, on the surface, add some semblance of validity to this claim:

General Appearance:

Unless the woman in labour can maintain Hollywood-style glamour throughout, she will look increasingly bedraggled as the hours go by. Even Pamela Anderson must have looked a little rumpled on the day of her baby's delivery.

Hair:

The hair, especially, will take leave of its normal terms of reference. This could just be the most unkempt that the mother's hair will ever look. 'Windswept' does not even begin to describe the degree of untidiness likely to be on display.

Legs Akimbo:

Not only will the mother fail to look stunning, she will also find herself in all sorts of unattractive positions. In a room visited at various times by midwives, anaesthetists, consultants, junior doctors and, most annoyingly, prying medical students, the mother will be obliged to put her most private of features on open display. As if having legs akimbo were not enough of an indignity, the features being revealed will, at various stages, appear messy, distorted and, finally, stretched to the limit.

Demeanour:

In addition to the lack of physical charm, the mother's temperament may also manifest itself in an unwelcome manner. Tiredness will reduce her ability to smile gently upon all the frustrations, irritations, and complications pertaining to the experience. Screaming and swearing are widely regarded as being 'par for the course', and husbands are warned well in advance to expect a bumpy ride.

All of these characteristics may manifest themselves, but it would be a very poor husband indeed to blame his wife for being dishevelled at a time like this. There is really no call for the husband to add to the indignity and the pain by casting a critical gaze upon his wife. If a man is bothered by his woman's physical appearance, or if her predicament becomes a matter of disgust, then there must be something wrong with his code of values.

Appreciation

It is more likely that the man will feel an overwhelming sense of gratitude to the woman who is undergoing such a terrific ordeal in order to give birth to the next member of the family. The idea of seeing a woman at her worst in this context is rather laughable. If anything, the opposite applies, in that what the man actually witnesses is a tremendous act of dedication and self-sacrifice. The virtue attached to the mother's willingness to undergo such a hardship is simply immeasurable – that is, assuming that she previously had some idea of what she was letting herself in for. But then, I have never met a mother who did not realize the implications of the original act of penetration.

With all this in mind, it seems more appropriate to say that a man who attends the bedside during labour will be seeing his wife during her finest hour. Better make that 'finest eighteen hours'. Not all the scenes will be pretty, but many scenes will be pretty amazing, and most will also be beautifully unselfish.

Follow-up Presentation

Later on, when the baby has been born and is becoming more than a handful at home, there will be many times when the mother will struggle to come to terms with the idea of making herself look presentable as well as looking after the baby. At such times, the man might just possibly be tempted to allow himself to think that he is *now* seeing his woman at her worst. Take such a view if you wish, but bear in mind that such an appraisal of one's partner is not only mean-spirited, it also completely misses the point. The point being, of course, that you will only find the worst if you really look for it.

13

DIVERSIONS

Diverted Male

Within the initial stages, moments of excitement, such as the splashing of water, are fairly few and far between. Of course, labour is not meant to be an opportunity for excitement and voyeurism. The partner's role is based around providing care and loving support for the mother-to-be. Nevertheless, there will be periods when the partner is required simply to be there, and not necessarily to be playing an active role in the process. It is likely that the midwife will be buzzing around, doing all the necessary chores and simultaneously putting the mother-to-be at her ease. During these times, you will need some form of diversion. Watching television may be an acceptable option, but it is more likely to be an intrusion. The same applies to listening to music. Catching up on your sleep will not go down well, and you may not be able to control when you wake up. All of these options will send out the wrong signals, i.e. that you would rather be somewhere else, and that you cannot be relied upon to play the required supporting role.

In my experience, the best solution was to attack *The Times* crossword. This activity provided a marvellous opportunity for intellectual stimulation, whilst at the same time it afforded the option to break off whenever appropriate, in order to revert back to the main event. The intensity of the situation seemed ideal for concentrating the mind, and, consequently, clue-solving was remarkably easy. This was so much the case that within a period of a little more than an hour and a half, I completed not just the main crossword but also the concise crossword, and I came within one answer of also completing the weekend jumbo cryptic crossword. To my mind, that was an astonishing performance, given the fact that normally, the jumbo takes the best part of a week, on and off, with constant delving into dictionaries and other works of reference. Furthermore, doing the crossword is normally a joint endeavour with my wife. There, in the delivery room, Angela showed no desire to be involved, with her mind being on other matters, for some reason. She later told me that she had not really been aware of what I had been doing during those moments when I had not been actively participating and immediately by her side.

Diverted Female

Whilst the father-to-be is merrily entertaining himself with a range of diversions, the mother-to-be will steadily continue to undergo the process of labour. The ultimate aim of having the cervix dilate to a diameter of ten centimetres can seemingly take forever to achieve. In the meantime, if pain relief has not already been administered, then it will come higher and higher up the agenda as the contractions increase.

There are six main options when it comes to seeking relief from pain.

1) Entonox (also known as gas and air)
Comes out of a mask applied to the face; similar to emergency oxygen masks to be found on board aeroplanes. The mixture of gas and air induces drowsiness, but the effects are short-lived, and will probably not offer sufficient relief to handle the big contractions. As another form of diversion, husbands tend to have a sneaky drag of Entonox when the midwife is not looking. I tried this, but didn't feel any

change in my state of being. Perhaps my technique was all wrong.

2) TENS machine (Transcutaneous Electrical Nerve Stimulation, for the uninitiated)

Available from high-street chemists and various other outlets, TENS machines act on the principle of applying gentle pressure to various parts of the body, in order to deflect the woman's attention away from the really painful areas.

3) Pethidine

Usually the second form of relief administered after it has been found that Entonox does not really do the trick. Even this drug-based relief does not really take the pain away. It merely makes the woman feel drowsy, and therefore less aware of the pain that is still being brought on by the contractions. A potential drawback to using this drug is that it has the ability to flow through the umbilical cord, and can thus make the baby as drowsy as the mother. Timing is crucial, since a baby should not be feeling woozy when the time comes to make its way out along the birth canal.

4) Epidural

The only option that really takes the pain away. Pain may still persist if the anaesthetist does not manage to hit the right spot, but usually, the probability of total pain relief is fairly high. However, the standard epidural has the side effect of numbing the mother from the waist down. This is fine whilst the cervix is still dilating. When it comes to the big push, the epidural is not regarded in such a good light. Since the woman is numb in the main area of play, establishing a pattern of pushing can be extremely difficult. Moreover, once the baby is out, and all the mess cleared up, the mother should remember that any attempt at going for a stroll will result in collapsing into a heap on the floor. Several hours must elapse before full sensation is recovered.

5) *Acupuncture*

The process of having needles stuck into areas of the body that are not even in pain. Dainty, gentle needles that work magic. Popular with progressive, holistic types, and hence still fairly uncommon. I find it hard to understand how acupuncture can work, but a cousin of mine recently took this option and was immediately impressed by the results.

6) *No artificial pain relief at all*

Judging from the number and the intensity of screams that we could hear from adjacent delivery suites, it is evident that having little or no artificial pain relief is a desirable option for a significant proportion of women in labour.

Grin and Bear It

In the earlier section describing the onset of labour, I explained how a man could be forgiven for wanting his wife to feel pain, since pain would indicate that things were finally happening. The same could just apply, although to a lesser degree, in the advanced stages of labour; the justification here being that an increase in pain might suggest that the moment of delivery was approaching.

Moreover, it is not unknown for a woman to want to undergo the 'total' labour experience. By this, I refer to the practice of going through labour without using any form of artificially induced pain relief. The following reasons might explain why an expectant mother might want to go down this route:

1) A genuine ability to withstand pain.
2) A misguided belief in the ability to withstand pain.
3) An ascetic sense of duty.
4) A fear of any possible side effects, to the baby or self.
5) A feeling that labour would not really be authentic without pain.

6) An appreciation of the importance of preserving the age-old tradition of screaming.

Whatever the woman's motives, the man should be wholly supportive of her choice. Such support is commendable, as long as it does not encompass the belief that his wife is embracing pain with open arms. It is one thing to be brave in the face of pain, and quite another thing to positively welcome pain.

Ringing in Your Ears

Having heard the screams from along the corridor, I cannot imagine any justification for criticizing a woman in labour for taking any form of pain relief. Conversely, I would expect any man to encourage anything that might comfort his wife throughout the ordeal. If for no other reason, he will not wish to be sworn at or be abused by her in any other way. Women in labour are notorious for getting angry with their husbands. Women's behaviour can be outrageously out of character under these circumstances.

If men, themselves, are not abused, then their wedding rings might be. Again, it has been known for women in pain to grip their husbands' hands so tightly that they end up putting the ring out of shape. Square wedding rings tend to look a bit silly. With these risks in mind, it is probably wise not to tell your wife to 'Grin and bear it'.

14

APPROACHING THE BIG MOMENT

The following sections relate to what I would call unusual deliveries, although the medical notes always claim that such deliveries are normal, whatever 'normal' may be when it comes to childbirth.

In the long lead-up to the final stages of delivery, right from parentcraft classes through to the last few minutes, you will probably expect that the baby will come out head first, through the usual combination of panting and pushing. However, there is always a possibility that complications will arise, leading to a change of plan on the part of both the baby and the midwife, and hence leading also to the involvement of doctors and consultants.

Compromising Positions

The term 'compromise' sounds like a reasonably helpful sort of expression, in that if the baby cannot come out the ideal way, it will compromise with you and come out the next best way. Used in the context of delivery, however, 'compromised' is not a word that you wish your baby to be associated with. Generally speaking, if a baby is compromised, then it may well be in some danger, however fleeting or easily remedied.

For the father-to-be, the best, perhaps the only sign that the baby is being compromised comes from the monitor at the side of the bed. This gadget gives either a numerical or a colour-based reading of the baby's heartbeat throughout the ordeal. A number between 70 and 150 is within acceptable parameters, as is the alternative of a green light. A number outside this range, or a red light, could, over a prolonged period, indicate a problem.

There are several key points to note here:

1) the reading will lose accuracy if the sensor slips out of position.
2) readings will be affected during contractions.
3) unless you press the medical staff on the point, they will probably not tell you how long is too long. Time is probably only important in the unlikely circumstance of the midwife disappearing without trace.
4) the monitor is merely an aid. As in nearly all other matters, the midwife is the key source of information. If something really is amiss, you will know from watching her, anyway.

Reasons for Instrumentation

Monitor readings are only one of the factors that can affect a doctor's decision to pick up an instrument. Generally, any circumstance that causes distress to the baby and/or the mother will influence a change to the plot. Even if distress cannot absolutely be established, there is always a potential for distress, and this may be sufficient for a change of course.

A common cause of such a change is the simple misalignment of the baby's head with the one available exit from the host body. Both our babies seemed unable to present themselves in an acceptable fashion, and both had to be assisted on their journey into the great outside.

Another is the time and effort already spent in what should be the final stage of delivery. Current practice is to allow a mother to push normally for up to an hour. If baby has not arrived by this time, then it will almost certainly need to be helped out.

The ultimate instrument is the scalpel, of course, but all available options will be explored fully before the need arises to consider taking such drastic action.

Instrumental Deliveries

Both of our children were delivered with a little instrumental assistance. Whilst the two events were remarkably similar, the choice of implements on each occasion provided me with a range of diverse images and experiences.

1) Forceps

My experience of watching a doctor in action with a pair of forceps was really quite challenging. Positioned at the side of the bed, I had a grandstand view of a quite remarkable exposition of manual dexterity and scientific technique. All the same, however clever the procedure, it still did not seem quite right; a) because of the potential for errors, and b) because I had always imagined that the baby would come out on its own accord, albeit with a little pushing and panting on the part of my wife.

As I surveyed the action, it struck me that my baby's head could be likened to a sugar cube that was being manipulated with a giant pair of metal sugar tongs. One significant difference was that a sugar cube is an entity in itself, whereas a baby's head is attached to a body that must also be treated with great care. Another image that flashed through my mind was that of a button mushroom covered in oyster sauce, held precariously between a set of chopsticks. It is extraordinary how one's mind wanders at times like these.

All the while, I was also concerned with how Angela was bearing up. Even though she had had an epidural, and also a top-up to the epidural after the original shot had lost its effect, I still imagined that there might be some significant pain involved. The doctor's use of the scissors in performing a complimentary episiotomy added to my overall view that the delivery was not progressing as smoothly as I could have hoped, and that there might be subsequent difficulties, even when the baby had long since been delivered. Looking back, I suppose it was standard practice for the doctor to open things up a bit, to allow more room to manoeuvre with the forceps.

Oblivious to all my concerns, and given all this gentle persuasion, baby came out happily enough, and we were all delighted.

2) The Ventouse

Our second child was also destined to come out with a little instrumental help. Despite the experience of having previously watched a forceps delivery, the appearance of a ventouse again threatened to upset my composure. Still, I was confident that this doctor would also know how to handle his equipment. (He later told me that he had performed hundreds of similar deliveries, so I need not really have been concerned.). Maintaining a typically British stiff upper lip, I watched the precision-skilled operation with fascination.

If you have never seen a ventouse, then imagine a shallow metal cup, smaller in diameter than a baby's head, with a suction hose attached to it. The technique basically involves sucking the baby out with the aid of a vacuum. Given that the ventouse fits so tightly to the head, it is little wonder that bruising occurs. It is unpleasant, but normal to see the head become somewhat misshapen during the process. Despite knowing that the head will revert to its proper shape within a few days, it is worrying to see it being squashed and pulled about. For a few horrid instants, the force applied in the extraction looked as if it might just be great enough to separate the head from the body. Thankfully, the baby soon made a complete and healthy exit from his mother. My relief was immense. I supposed that baby must have felt even more relieved.

Without realizing it, I must have revealed all these concerns in my countenance. This effect must have been augmented by the sense of awe and wonder that I was feeling, on being present – for the second time – at the scene of a truly spectacular and marvellous happening. Perhaps recognizing all of these feelings in my face, the doctor and midwife asked me on several occasions if I was feeling all right. After about the third time of asking, I felt slightly bemused by the concern for me, when it was my wife who was at the centre of the action. It was later suggested to me that the concern of the medical staff might have been less for my well-being, and more out of a wish not to see me swoon and cause even more complications during an already complex procedure. Anyway, I was fine throughout. It obviously just didn't look that way.

15

THE MOMENT OF DELIVERY

I have always tended to believe that whilst men are allowed to cry, and even to cry in public, there is still something inside of me that makes me want to suppress such a manifestation of deep, heartfelt emotion. On some occasions, the urge to express tears can be so strong, but rarely as strong as it was on this occasion. For a few moments, I realized that I was prepared to let myself go, and I really wanted to allow my eyes to behave in a manner fitting to the circumstances, but somehow my subconscious sense of asceticism prevented me from spilling any tears.

Soon after, it was pointed out that it had looked as if I was going to cry, and I acknowledged the validity of the observation. I even felt a little pleased that I had not actually betrayed my subconscious machismo. Strange, since the process of becoming a father surely allows the manifestation of joy in any way that feels suitable.

Mixed Emotions

The birth of a child can arouse all kinds of feelings, some individual, some shared. In my case, I remember feeling a combination of relief, happiness, satisfaction, and smugness. Relief, in that we had all pulled through unscathed. Happiness, in experiencing a joy that surpassed even the thrill of England winning the Ashes in 1985. Satisfaction, in realizing our dream of becoming a family. Smugness, in knowing that I had made a major contribution to the creation of this wonderful new being. The seed that I had planted some nine months previously had finally come to fruition quite splendidly.

Ending With a Toast to the New Beginning

Just as pregnancy and labour have come to an end, so a new life has just begun. Moreover, a new family, or an increase in the size of an existing family has just been confirmed.

To celebrate the new beginning, it is customary for the proud parents to be presented with toast and coffee. This happens in Slough, and probably in many other places, too. In Middlesbrough, I am informed, the breakfast consists of *tea* and coffee. Whatever the drink, I cannot help but observe that this seems like a rather mundane breakfast to follow the extraordinary previous goings on. I can remember that eating toast was the last thing on my mind, and really quite an unappetizing prospect. Nevertheless, even if you do not partake of the offering, the kindness of the midwife is to be noted.

Taking It All In

Following all the razzmatazz surrounding the delivery, it is important to spend some quiet time together, undisturbed by the hospital staff. This will offer the chance to begin contemplating everything that has just happened. A few minutes of absolute tranquillity can be priceless. In times to come, moments of peace will be rare.

Breaking the News

Having enjoyed some quiet moments together as a family, there is now yet another special task to perform. The chance to pass on some truly happy information does not come along all that often, and it really is a pleasure to be the bearer of glad tidings. Assuming that there are people sitting by the telephone, or even asleep waiting to be woken up, then tell them as soon as you are ready. Even though no one else will have gone through exactly what you have gone through during the labour, they will probably have experienced their own private anguish. They will be relieved and delighted to know what has happened.

Snappiness after the Event

Shortly after the toast and coffee, the father may well feel like getting out the camera to record the very early stages of the baby's life. In some cases, a camcorder may even be brought out. Now, I reckon that you can miss more than you gain by being behind a camcorder. Having to concentrate on making a movie can easily take away from the wider interests of the moment, and will cause you to focus on only one element of a much more expansive scene. Moreover, the presence of a camcorder will almost certainly prove unwelcome to the mother. Still photographs, in turn, are also potentially intrusive, but the taking of them can be limited to an instant, or a series of instants. When push comes to shove, determined photographers will usually feel more than justified in capturing on film an event that can never be recreated.

The uniqueness of the moment will encourage the proud father to take a number of set pieces. Suitable cameos include the baby being hosed down, the baby being passed over to the mother for the first time, and the baby being put to the breast for a first-ever feed. Another popular shot is the family trio, to be taken by a co-operative midwife. Such scenes seem reasonable to the father. The mother may well take a different view. She could easily object to being photographed at a time when she considers herself to be not quite at her best. Fathers: take note. Even though you may feel highly delighted by everything that has just happened, it is wise to imagine yourself in the position of the mother. In your continuing state of elation, you may simply fail to notice the ugly tubes connecting the drip solutions to the mother's back and arms. You may even fail to notice the look of utter exhaustion on your wife's face. Worse still, you may be oblivious to the fact that even though your wife has just unloaded some of her excess baggage, she still looks like a blob.

Still, some women genuinely do not mind being photographed under these conditions. They may consider it a beautiful sacrifice for the sake of posterity. Alternatively, they may simply not be concerned about how they look, since they are totally preoccupied by the marvellous little baby that has just arrived.

In extreme cases, photography may even be performed throughout the labour. Some enlightened parents feel comfortable enough to record even the most intimate of scenes. This includes close-ups of the female nether regions before, during, and after the emergence of the baby. In such cases, it can be assumed that the mother is in total agreement. You can only presume that she is keen to see, at some later stage, a representation of the event as seen from the father's point of view. I imagine that such pictures, when taken sensitively, must inspire fond memories for the father, and a precious insight for the mother. Nevertheless, the idea of taking pictures at such an intimate level of detail must seem bizarre to many couples.

Pictures of the exhibition should provide the parents with a lifetime of visual memory aids. Budding photographers may even regard pictures taken during labour as constituting their magnum opus. Having said this, I must return to the importance of not spending too much time taking pictures. Several years ago, a friend from Down Under, appropriately enough, took what he considered would be a marvellous, comprehensive series of confidential shots that would form a lasting image of a hugely emotional event. This seemed fine, up until the point when he subsequently

73

lent the camera to another friend, who made the terrible mistake of rewinding the film and then double-exposing it. An unforeseeable occurrence, perhaps, but nonetheless heartbreaking for being so. I just hope that my Kiwi friend took time out to peep out from behind the viewfinder from time to time.

Pain, But No Regrets

It is not unheard of for women to vow to remain childless because they do not wish, or dare, to endure the pain incurred during childbirth. I do not offer a judgement in this matter. I will just refer to Angela's attitude towards pain, which she explained to me six months after the birth of our second child.

The main thrust of her argument was that whilst she had not enjoyed the pain on either occasion, she did not regret having suffered. Nor did she resent any aspect of the plight in which she had come to find herself. Conversely, she went on to outline the benefits that are to be gained by experiencing labour pains. Suffering, she claimed, made her feel even more involved. Without pain, it might easily have been possible to feel somewhat detached from the action. Moreover, her pain also allowed me, her supportive husband and birth partner, to feel more involved myself. This was justified on the grounds that by seeing her in pain, I was bound to produce an emotional response.

Overall, her point was that even though pain in labour is distressing, it can also enrich the experience of bringing a new life into being. Marvellous! I consider this to be an extraordinarily enlightened and unselfish approach to a fascinating subject.

74

16

MORE HOSPITAL NOTES

Hospital Staff

During a spell in hospital, a whole range of members of staff will cross your path. Most of them will be absolutely marvellous. Midwives, in particular, are wonderfully gifted people who help to make the experience so much easier.

The main players include, roughly in order of appearance, all or most of the following:

*nurses/midwifery sisters/house doctors/registrars/
consultants/porters/delivering midwives/anaesthetists/
paediatricians.*

Accentuated Difficulties

For the husband in particular, there is at least one other hospital employee who may play a key role. I hardly ate anything during the whole weekend covering the birth of my first child, but I was rather keener to take in some nourishment on the occasion of the birth of number two. Since the hospital meal trolleys do not tend to provide for husbands, I found myself wandering around Wexham Park Hospital in search of a substantial bite to eat.

This is not significant in itself. I mention it merely because I was afforded a good deal of jollity by a German lady serving behind the counter of the cafeteria. When I asked her the about the nature of a certain item covered in breadcrumbs, she replied that it was called 'wheel'. After several repeats of the question and the answer, I finally realized that the dish on offer was actually Wiener Schnitzel. Whilst such trifling cases of mispronunciation might not seem all that funny after the event, and certainly they are trivial in the context of an imminent labour, I found this episode really rather amusing. This exchange added a light-hearted touch to a long, drawn-out, and otherwise strenuous period of waiting. It also confirmed my misgivings about allowing non-English-speaking Europeans to come over here and be rewarded with such positions of responsibility.

Early Days and More Fears

In the first section of the book, I included a list of fears that a father-to-be may develop within the course of a pregnancy. A lot of those early fears will already have been overcome – largely on seeing the baby successfully delivered. Now, in the first few days of baby's fragile existence, a whole new list of fears presents itself:

1) The fear that baby will be stolen from the hospital. Increased security systems are now in operation, but no amount of tagging and video surveillance can keep away a really determined baby snatcher.
2) The fear that baby will be swapped, accidentally or otherwise, with another baby in the hospital. There is an outside chance of ending up with someone else's pride and joy, and of that someone else receiving one's own precious creation.
3) The fear of not knowing how to cope without the help of the hospital staff.
4) The fear of having an accident on the journey home.

As with the first list of fears, this list is not exhaustive. Any number of niggling worries and major concerns may creep into the mind. The trick is to blot them out, to take all reasonable precautions, and to assume the confidence that will constantly be necessary from this point onwards.

The Voyage Home

Departing

Taking mother and baby home from the hospital can be an affair highly charged with emotion. There will probably be a mixture of relief and anxiety. Relief, in that you can finally wave goodbye to the hospital; and anxiety, in that baby is about to be taken out into a totally different and more challenging environment. However much you may prepare for this first journey, it still comes as quite a shock to realize that you must suddenly assume a great deal more responsibility. Up until the point where you step outside the maternity ward, the responsibility for mother and baby is largely due to the sisters and the nurses. Once outside the hospital, ultimate responsibility passes to the father.

As protector of the family, your first task may well be to shield the infant from the smoke puffed into the air immediately outside the entrance door, where gasping patients and visitors gather for a cigarette. Having overcome the challenge of preventing baby from suffering an early bout of passive smoking, the next task is to secure the baby in the car. Nowadays, the standard means of baby conveyance involves the use of a specially designed car seat. At this early stage, baby will look incredibly small in the seat. You will probably want to capture the image on film, to remind yourself, later on in life, of exactly how tiny babies really are when they are born.

There are many different baby car seats on the market, but they all seem to share one basic property: they are never easy for the first-time parent to install. For some, the task of belting up baby can be more than a little frustrating. This may not be the fault of the seat, but perhaps of the car, instead. Some cars do not even provide enough seat belt to secure the seat according to the manufacturer's reasonable instructions. This may mean having to change the belt, at the risk of invalidating the warranty, or even changing the car, if this proves to be a better option. Typically, problems like this are discovered only when it comes to taking baby home for the first time, and this can make things very awkward.

Assuming that you have overcome any difficulties, not the least of which being the decision as to whether to face baby in a forward- or rear-facing position, it is then time to begin the drive home. For the parents, this will involve travelling along the familiar road home. For baby, the car ride will be a journey into undiscovered country, although sleep is likely to deprive baby of some of the excitement. In both cases, the trip can be regarded as a hugely symbolic rite of passage. This could be summed up as the family embarking together, not just on a short trip home, but on the first stage of a lifelong voyage through life.

Romulans on the Starboard Bow

In *Star Trek* terms, going home from the hospital in a Volkswagen Golf is somewhat akin to leaving a star base in order to return to the *Enterprise* on board a humble shuttle craft. In both cases, neither modes of transport seem particularly sturdy. Traversing Windsor Great Park is similar to tripping through the Neutral Zone. The outlook can be bleak, and there are no welcoming sights along the way. Safety is only to be attained by overcoming a host of potentially hostile forces, including cloaked Romulan war birds (unmarked police cars) and ugly Cardassians (road rage monsters), along the route. Only once home, either in the house or on board a galaxy-class starship, can the family really begin to interact.

Arriving Home

There is nothing quite as satisfying as bringing baby home for the first time. The feeling of joy will be far greater than the excitement felt on bringing in a new kitten, or a favourite Chinese takeaway meal, or a new Denon hi-fi midi system, or a new Nicam stereo Panasonic video recorder (with PDC), or anything else. Having a baby in the home means so much. A leading journalist for *The Times* once stated that he decided to have children because he lived in the sort of home where, he thought, children might like to grow up. I like to think that this scenario applies in our house, too. Providing a space for an additional member of the family is one of the earliest joys of parenthood.

Hopefully, you will have prepared for the new arrival. The welcoming of the baby into the family home need not be ceremonious, but it should be a happy and significant event. With help from friends and relatives, there may even be colour-coded balloons on display, to add an element of festivity to the occasion. Little touches like this may not mean much to the baby himself, but they do add to the special nature of the event. Having baby's brothers and sisters (if there are any) eagerly anticipating the arrival of the little bundle makes an even more meaningful impact.

Enjoy the moment. A house alive to the crying of a baby at three o'clock in the morning will subsequently make the home feel slightly less idyllic.

PART 3

Following On

17

HOME DEVELOPMENT

Bursting the Balloon

In the days and weeks following the arrival at home, countless good wishes and gestures of support will come flooding in. The trouble is, such offers of kindness can become oppressive. It does not take much for people to get on top of each other and for arguments to begin. Before long, the situation can leave you gasping for air and generally trying to survive, whilst still attempting to enjoy the precious early stages in the development of the baby.

With this in mind, spend a little time before the birth deciding how you both wish to see things operate once mother and baby have come home. Advice will be plentiful, but possibly inconclusive. Some will advise on taking full advantage of every offer of help; others will suggest keeping other people (including close family) away for a few days, to allow a little breathing space. The answer may not be easy to come by.

The following passages reveal the opinions of a man who is occasionally prone towards bouts of grumpiness. Hence, the views expressed will certainly not apply universally. However, I do feel that they will have some relevance for everyone.

In-laws are notorious for stepping in and offering assistance in abundance. But then, one partner's in-laws are the other partner's parents, and vice versa. A great deal of sensitivity needs to be employed, and sensitivity under these circumstances is not always readily at hand. In this context, tolerance is not always a strong enough characteristic. Getting through it all unscathed is out of the question. The only solution is to accept that times will be extremely demanding, and that other people will not be easy to get along with, and that hurting is simply one of the inescapable side effects of having to interact within the family. Coming to terms with the difficulties, and trying to do everything possible to minimize them, is all important. The expression 'water off a duck's back' is rather simplistic, but it does suggest the best way of handling any unwelcome contretemps.

Jealousy and Selfishness

One of the main reasons for reacting badly to offers of help is the simple human tendency towards jealousy. For a father, particularly a first-time father, it is only natural to want to spend as much time as possible with mother and child. He will want to be useful, but this does not go nearly far enough. He will want to be the *most* useful helper within the home. Instinctively, the father will seek to become the second most significant presence in the new baby's life. The mother will take pride of place, but after her, no one else should come between father and child. Such a desire will burn within the father's heart during the baby's formative weeks, and possibly for some considerable time afterwards.

Quite simply, this desire is grounded in having become used to being an equal half of the procreating partnership. It is a continuation of all of the feelings and desires experienced during pregnancy and labour. Anyone who challenges this position of dominance within the family set-up is an immediate threat. Strong language, perhaps, but humans can be fairly basic, and the primeval instincts are never far away. The common reaction to the perceived threat is irascible behaviour. It may come across in a variety of ways. Rattiness, impatience, intolerance; they are all expressions of displeasure, aimed at trying to re-establish dominance within any given situation.

Selfishness, of course, is at the root of such behaviour. Crack the secret of always putting other people first, and you will be laughing. Still, bear in mind that the decision to have a baby was, in the first place, almost certainly based on some regard for the self. Considering the self is not necessarily wrong. It merely becomes wrong when the self becomes an all-consuming preoccupation. In most cases, fathers will stop short of obsessive behaviour, but there will always be an element of wanting to be Number One.

Learning to cope with being selfish, and trying to overcome simple human disagreements within a framework acceptable to all parties concerned, is one of the hardest challenges that you will face when bringing up baby. It is also the most immediate challenge. Lifestyles obviously have to change. How they change is where the fun starts.

The Greenhouse Effect

Once the initial excitement of bringing the baby home has died down, a number of opportunities for disagreement will arise fairly quickly. An immediate concern will be the temperature level within the home. It is highly likely that the mother and father will have strongly conflicting views on the appropriate indoor climate. As a general rule, the father will regard the normal temperature inside the house as being satisfactorily warm, and the mother will have a quite different opinion. The perception of warmth may well be affected by the time of year, but this is not always the case.

Understandably, the mother will be acclimatized to the subtropical temperatures of the hospital that she has just left behind, and the father will be used to what he considers to be normal living conditions. Both parties will feel fully justified in making a demand for changes to the thermostat according to their respective positions. The mother, on her part, may well try to persuade the father that the baby needs to live in abnormally warm conditions, although she may not even consider her preferred temperature to be abnormal. The father, on his part, will find it hard not to suggest that such conditions make it feel like living in a greenhouse.

There are plenty of points that need to be considered here. For starters, the woman's body will still be adjusting to the unusual circumstances. She will initially be less active, since rest is important, and hence will generate less warmth. Hormones will continue to change and will cause varying effects on the body. This naturally includes the perception of temperature. Moreover, given that the mother will spend long periods when her clothes will be undone to allow the baby to suckle on the breast, it is perfectly reasonable for her to expect that this state of affairs will be compensated for by an increase in the room temperature.

Faced with increasingly stifling conditions, the father is presented with a number of options:

1) Counteract the sweltering conditions by wearing a T-shirt and shorts. This may seem like a simple option, although it can have the wrong effect if the mother interprets such mode of apparel as an act of sarcasm.

2) Take every opportunity to go outside the house, in order to escape the oppressive artificial environment. This is not always feasible, even if it is desirable, especially if there is no one else around to look after the mother and child.

3) Purchase a simple room thermometer, and consult it frequently in an attempt to apply some scientific basis for argument. However, scientific evidence is almost bound to play second fiddle to the mother's own sensory perceptions.

4) Finally, pick the right moment to open a window. When this act of foolishness has been discovered, impress upon the mother how you were merely trying

to bring some fresh air into the house, rather than trying to lose the warmth. The explanation won't wash, but at least it will help prevent you from appearing to be deliberately unhelpful.

It is easy to see the link between rising temperatures and rising tempers. As in all matters of dispute, a solution has to be found. Bearing in mind all the explanatory factors noted above, it is wise and sensible to try and fit in with the mother's wishes wherever possible. Be prepared to be accused of wanting the house to be like an icebox. You will know that this is nonsense, but it doesn't really hurt to be accused in this way.

Feeling for Clues

If you really must seek justification for demanding a change to the thermostat, then the best point of reference will come from an assessment of the baby's own level of comfort. This will be affected by the room temperature; the ideal being around 65° to 70° Fahrenheit. A thermometer can never be relied on absolutely, however, especially if it is a cheap cardboard-and-plastic model from a well-known baby outfitters. A number of factors may affect the accuracy of such a reading, and therefore the legitimacy of your arguments in favour of a change up or down.

The most meaningful·indication as to whether or not the baby is too warm can, in fact, be gained by feeling the baby's tummy. This may not sound a very precise technique, but baby matters rarely are precise. There is always an element of parental discretion. The difficulty is compounded when the two parents insist on different levels of discretion. Knowing how to resolve such matters can only come from experience, and not always then.

A final word on this matter. This kind of difference of opinion is just the start of a whole range of real and potential difficulties that will need to be surmounted. It is a good idea for the man, especially, to learn to be patient, and to accept conditions that are not immediately to his liking, in order to fall into a habit of being unselfish. After all, the mother has many more immediate concerns to deal with, without having to take part in a conflict that could otherwise be avoided. Putting someone else first, at personal cost, is a fundamental feature of relationships within the family. Even if you consider yourself to be in the right, it helps enormously to grin and bear the wishes of your loved ones.

Postnatal Blues

Postnatal depression is the term generally used to describe a new mother's inexplicable bouts of sadness during the days and weeks immediately following the birth. Generally, the depression is short-lived and not very deep. Some mothers do not even suffer from it at all. In contrast, extreme cases of depression have led to mothers completely rejecting their offspring.

Fathers, for their part, must sit back and wait to see how the depression will manifest itself. This should not, of course, involve constant scrutiny of the mother's state of being. Placing the mother's behaviour under a psychological microscope will hardly help matters. In any case, nothing may happen.

In the case of our first child, the only sign of sadness came during lunch, a few days after arriving home from hospital. Halfway through a dish of heavily garlicked chicken and potatoes, Angela suddenly burst out into a flood of tears. After a few brief moments, the tears ceased. Even this spontaneous display of emotion may not have been due to traditional postnatal depression, since I seem to remember having behaved like a pig to her on that particular day. On the occasion of our second child, I cannot recall even one incident of mystery madness. Perhaps Angela was simply too level-headed to play ball with the conventional stereotype. Alternatively, perhaps any evidence of sadness was so minuscule and short-lived that it went by unnoticed.

Within my own experience, I suffered from a male form of postnatal depression very soon after becoming a father for the first time. Following the tremendous feeling of elation that same morning, I could not help but feel just a little bit deflated on later learning that Manchester City had finally been relegated from the Premiership. I was helped along in this matter no end by friends who were quick to point out the hilarious irony in the fact that both my team and my baby had dropped on the very same day.

Curiously enough, only a few months after the dropping of child number two, City slipped down yet another division. How spooky is that? To go down one flight is bad enough, but to go down two within the space of three years is quite a considerable vexation. I like coincidences, and I like patterns in life, but does the huge thrill of becoming a father really have to go hand in hand with this kind of let-down?

(As I apply a few finishing touches to this book, City have already leapt back up into the first division – thanks to the five very dodgy minutes of extra time in the 1999 play-off final at Wembley – and are now poised to reclaim their rightful place in the Premiership. City: perennial winners of the Cup for Cock-ups, or Pride of Manchester? One thing I am convinced of is that a third baby could see the Blues returning once again to the nether regions. For the sake of all long-suffering City followers, the decent thing must be for me to refrain from having any more children. I cannot promise that!).

Avoiding the Issue

Visiting midwives and health visitors can be very supportive. They can also seem more than a little intrusive. On top of asking the expected questions about baby's progress, they will also reel off some standard questions related to how babies are made. One key question is what type of contraception to use once carnal relations resume. At such an early stage, sex will probably be way down the list of things to do, and the libido will not be much in force anyway. Hence, any inquiries into such matters will not only be a little unwelcome, they will also be irrelevant, at least for the time being. The best response to such quizzing is to let the mother make a joke about never letting the father come near her again. This generally gets round the awkwardness, and directs the attention onto other topics. The most important thing for the moment is to realize that whilst family life is initiated by the process of coupling, there is so much more to it than that.

18

CHANGING TIMES

If the father does not get the chance to change nappies in the hospital, then the opportunity will arrive soon enough at home. 'Opportunity' is not really the right word here; changing nappies is an obligation, for whoever happens to be in the best position to do so at the time. This simple division of labour can break down if one party always mysteriously manages to be unavailable. Basically, for Ben Elton's favourite creature, the post-modern ironic man, there is no reasonable escape.

Changing nappies is not really all that bad – at least, not if the contents are dry and minimal, the change takes place during the day, and the action has to be performed only once. Sounds fair. But, babies are not fair. There are circumstances when nappy changing can be a really horrible business. Such circumstances include: a nappy full of runny excrement that has slopped over the side and contaminated the baby's clothes; a time of three o'clock in the morning; a need to perform change after change after change in quick succession, because baby just cannot stop relieving himself every time the latest clean nappy is applied. Yuck!

As you might expect, experiences vary from baby boys to baby girls. Boys, of course, are much more adept at aiming a spurt of urine in any chosen direction. Usually, they don't bother to aim, and just start spurting indiscriminately. When it comes to squirting liquid excrement, both sexes are equally skilled. The range and power of the squirt can be extraordinary, especially when triggered by a dish of prunes. Be warned!

Freebies

In the first few months of the baby's life, and in some cases for some considerable time afterwards, all sorts of free gifts and special offers will come through the post. Do not dismiss them lightly. A packet of one free mini-sized Pampers nappy may not seem much, but it might prove invaluable if your normal supply has temporarily been exhausted. In addition to free single nappies, both Huggies and Pampers send out money-off vouchers. Again, you might be tempted to sneer, since an occasional pound off a pack that normally costs £11 does not seem that much of a reduction. However, for each baby, the total value of nappy vouchers received is likely to be in excess of £50.

Vouchers are sent out for a whole host of diverse products, so the total of all discounts really could be quite significant. In addition to the vouchers, several leading stores offer free boxes of sample products. Other offers include free photographic portrait deals, free magazines, and free cassettes with magazines. Of course, we all know what free promotions lead to, but the rest depends on self-control. The old adage applies: never look a gift horse in the mouth. Equally, never let a gift horse take you for a ride.

A Shock to the System

Easy Beginnings

Babies, on the whole, have an easy life. Babies do not have to work for a living. Babies do not have to pick up a knife and fork to eat their meals; food comes regularly from a teat applied to the gums. Babies do not even have to wash themselves. Getting dressed is hardly more of an imposition. Babies do not have to visit Mothercare and M&S to buy their glad rags. They do not have to browse through the Next directory or the Jojo Maman Bébé catalogue. In fact, they scarcely have to lift a little finger in order to look after themselves. Somebody else does it all for them.

Whoever said that your schooldays are the best days of your life must have forgotten what it was like to be an infant. No homework to do for an undeserving teacher; no mortgage to tie you down to a humdrum job; no stress; no washing up. Succumbing to sleep is about as taxing as it gets.

Pointed Experiences

Life always throws up surprises, and some of them will be unpleasant. For a baby, the first really unpleasant surprises are the short, sharp, pointed shocks that are administered with needles. The first of these rude awakenings takes place shortly after birth, in the form of a shot of vitamin K and in a BCG vaccine to protect against TB. A few days into the baby's life, a Guthrie's test, comprising a series of unsuspected pricks, will be performed. The extracted blood is then sent off and used in a test to check that the baby is breaking down its milk properly. A sample of the blood is also used in a test for HIV, although results of this are only provided on request.

All goes quiet for two months, and then it is time for baby to undergo a three-month course of HIB injections to protect against diphtheria, tetanus, and whooping cough. To add insult to injury, the nurse follows up each jab with an anti-polio squirt down the throat, made easy by the fact that baby is still bawling away in protest against the nasty needle.

Once baby is at least a year old, and long after the HIBs have been forgotten, the next cocktail to be offered up is a dose of the combined MMR (measles, mumps, and rubella) vaccine. For all but the bravest of babies, the tears, if not the memories of previous pain, come flooding back.

Pricking One's Conscience

Vaccinations are not compulsory, of course. Parents may choose not to have their precious offspring treated thus for any number of reasons, valid or otherwise. You could argue that since everyone else has their children vaccinated, there is no need for your own to be protected. This assumption is huge, and only potentially valid. Some consider that the risk of detrimental side effects makes vaccination unacceptable. The current scare stories about MMR are a case in point.

On the whole, I am persuaded that the risks involved in not having the vaccinations far outweigh the risks involved in having them. Nevertheless, it is important to give the matter serious consideration. It is all too easy to flock to the clinic and to allow a stranger to puncture one's beloved children with a needle, simply because that is what is recommended. Doctors and nurses perform the service in the best interests of their patients, but we have a duty to our children to know why they have to undergo this ordeal. Distress may be necessary, but the reasons for allowing this distress must be understood.

Further Clinical Matters

Partly out of curiosity, partly out of a sense of duty, a first baby will be subjected to frequent visits to the clinic. In addition to taking the weight and height of the baby and marking them down against the percentiles on the growth chart, the health visitor will want to be assured that things are generally going well. Her questions will cover feeding, sleeping, and any worries or questions that the parents might have. It is not uncommon for parents to keep quiet about certain concerns, perhaps fearing that the health visitor will respond disapprovingly or will offer some unwelcome advice. However hard you try to be a good parent, there is always a nasty suspicion that the health visitor might just be mean enough to confiscate one's baby on some petty charge of incompetence. My big sister used to refer to her health visitor as The Witch, and having now come across the species myself, I can understand why.

On top of the regular measuring sessions, various tests

are performed on the developing baby. One major event is the hearing test. This involves asking the baby to respond to an audible stimulus, usually a rattle or a bell shaken in various positions and with various levels of decibels. A quick swivel of the head in response to a tiny ringing is all it takes to assure everyone that baby's ears are fully functional.

The first-time father will want to be present not only for this kind of milestone, but also for much more routine experiences. He will feel, to begin with, that a trip to the clinic is a bit like a visit to the oracle. It may well be that in the early stages of fatherhood, doctors and health visitors know much more about babies' health matters than the first-time parent. However, one of the basic principles of parenthood is that most of the knowledge you need is based on common sense. There will always be exceptional times and circumstances, but sooner or later, parents come to know how to look after their own children. Finding things out for yourself and learning to apply your new-found knowledge is a far more enjoyable and valuable experience than constantly allowing someone else to take control.

Having witnessed the 'successful' development of the first child, you tend to assume that the next one will simply follow suit. When it comes to the second child, attending a repeat performance can seem like something of a chore. More often than not, it is the mothers who tend to find themselves tasked with accompanying subsequent little ones to the clinic.

If both parents feel relaxed about the development of their children, then the need to visit the clinic will be vastly reduced. Luckily for the second and subsequent babies, they will consequently be spared the regular rigmarole of having to strip off to be weighed. As long as the key check-up sessions are attended, staying away from the clinic is perfectly acceptable. It demonstrates a greater degree of confidence on the part of the parents. It will also benefit the children in that they will not have to consort with The Witch.

19

MOVING ON UP

Bonding and Alienation

There is no doubt about it; having a baby will change the way that you relate to other people. In some cases, the changes may open up a whole new area in terms of relationships; in others, you may find yourself losing touch with people, and that you no longer have the same values and interests. In contrasting ways, you will probably enjoy a sense of keeping up with the friends who have already had children, whilst at the same time realizing that you have become at least a little bit alienated from those who have not.

For some considerable time after the big event, you will experience any number of joys relating to your treasured offspring. This will include proudly passing round photographs, talking fondly and excitedly about even the most minor of baby-related activities, and generally behaving in a way that reveals that something major has recently happened to you.

The pleasure that this brings, however, will not be shared by everyone; at least, not to the same degree. Do not be surprised if people without children remark on how your face seems to adopt a silly smirk at the merest mention of baby matters, when you yourself think that you are simply reacting with understandable pleasure. Be prepared, also, for getting involved in complex arguments on the advantages and disadvantages of having children, and for ending up feeling that the emphasis is on you to justify your own position.

Overall, you will find yourself bonding with some people and becoming alienated from others. This may not necessarily be due to who has children and who does not; it is merely one of the more obvious possible reasons.

Standing Room Only

In terms of how a baby affects your life within the home, it is often the simple things that stand out. One of the most basic of differences between life before and after the birth is that you have to get used to standing up a lot more often. Babies do not allow their parents, especially their Daddies, to sit down and relax for anything more than a few minutes. Mummies are allowed a bit more time, since the babies recognize how much extra effort they put in. So, for fathers, any idea of holding the baby on one side and reading *The Times* on the other is totally out of the question. Having a quick look at Ceefax to check up on the County Championship scores is also disallowed. Coffee is generally drunk cold, or lukewarm at best. As for having a sandwich, well, if baby is not eating at the same time, then this, too, is not permissible. All of these daily habits can be performed, but if a sitting position is required, then baby will ensure that the sound of crying prevents any clarity of mind.

The simple solution is to forego all of these basic activities, and to stand up and walk around the room with baby until either you drop from exhaustion or the baby falls asleep. Be advised that baby is likely to stay the course longer. When you can no longer keep on your feet, sit down again, allow the crying to restart, and wait to see how Mummy responds.

Hiccuping for England

On one of those precious rare occasions that Georgina would actually allow us both to sit down for more than a few seconds, we happened to catch a few glimpses of a test match between England and India. This seemed to be a fine way of introducing my daughter to cricket, and she watched with considerable interest. The voice of Great-uncle Richie Benaud was obviously having a soothing effect. After a period considered long enough for Georgina to absorb the nuances of the game, I thought it time to try her out with a few questions. Whilst unable to fully comprehend the intricacies of the LBW law, she was clearly *au fait* with the difference between a googly and a flipper, and she even suggested that Hirwani should try bowling over the wicket.

Having gurgled away on the beauty of the late cut, Georgina was then asked to name her favourite player. The answer was loud and clear: 'HICK.' She repeated the same answer over and over, at regular intervals, and I could only marvel at her recognition of such a fine batsman. After a while, I offered Georgina a few sips of water from the wrong side of the cup, placed a cold key down her back, and finally burst a balloon. There was still no end to the constant repetition: 'Hick ... Hick ... Hick ... Hick.' Had Great-uncle Richie not made way for Geoffrey Boycott, I think she might have continued in this vein right up until stumps.

Between a Man and His Cricket

Before getting married, I was assured by my then fiancée that she would never dream of coming between her man and his cricket. That was music to my ears, and I felt fully justified in playing on nearly every Saturday throughout summer. As a gesture of unselfishness, I declined to play on Sundays. This situation happily continued after we tied the knot, although on several occasions I had to remind Angela of her pledge. Subsequent family weddings did enforce a few absences from the greensward, but my average did not seem to suffer.

Having a baby suddenly jeopardized a prominent and

glorious playing career. When there had once only been the two of us to consider, I had always been able to recall that promise. Now, with Georgina on the scene, together with all the responsibilities and privileges commensurate with the rank of parent, I could sense that my playing days were about to be restricted. I tried in vain to extend the promise, to suggest that it could be altered along the lines of '*My baby and I* could never come between *our* man and his cricket', but this was unfair. Georgina had never been party to the original agreement, and she certainly could not be expected to allow her Daddy to disappear every Saturday without at least a bit of a whimper.

On top of all this, I knew that it was a bit much to expect a mother to cope with a baby on her own, and that even though I could possibly have got away on a technicality, it would have been unkind and unreasonable.

Now, with two children, although only one really deserving of a place on the MCC waiting list, the prospect of turning out for Haste Hill more than a handful of times a season is looking considerably murky. Taking the whole family to a match has never really appealed. I would be too concerned about hitting a six that could land on the pram being pushed around the boundary. Besides, with Angela likely to be called away to organize the teas, who would supervise the children? So, I fear that the sound of leather on willow is to become a distant memory; either that, or I run the risk of missing out on some of the best of times. Maybe, when the children are old enough to pursue their own interests, Haste Hill might just be short one day, and desperate enough to allow an old codger to play for them again. Still, for the time being, not rain, not bad light, but offspring stops play.

The Confidence Factor

Enjoying your children is a huge blessing in itself, yet there are lots of indirect benefits that come from becoming a parent. For people who might otherwise be a little reserved, one of the great bonuses arises in having a ready-made topic of conversation, together with all the social opportunities that follow on therewith.

An obvious reason for an increase in confidence is that you will be able to spend time with other people without feeling that they are particularly interested in you, since they must be interested in your baby, instead. Conversely, your ego might well take a leap when you feel that people, particularly of the opposite sex, are actually paying you a compliment when they say how lovely your child is. You cannot help but feel flattered by comments such as 'Oh, your baby's really cute; just like his father.' The presence of the child provides both the opportunity for an indirect compliment, and the means for diffusing any embarrassment that might lead on from the kind words.

In a more general context, confidence will increase simply through having found the means to talk freely and extensively about a particular subject. This subject might be babies, at first, but there is no reason why the conversation should not lead onto other fields of interest. Not only does it become much easier to overcome the initial hurdle of starting up a conversation, it also provides the scope to move on to talk more openly about a whole range of interests.

Taken to an extreme, for a father who is no longer connected with the mother, there will be countless opportunities for attracting welcome female attention. It might seem scheming to use baby in this fashion, but it might also lead on to a great deal of happiness.

20

SLEEPLESS NIGHTS

When baby is still young, one of the most frequently asked questions is 'Is the baby sleeping through the night?'. A variation on this is 'I expect you're having a lot of sleepless nights, aren't you?'. Well, it can be a little tedious to have to answer this question over and over again. At times, I have responded a bit flippantly, claiming that whenever I hear the baby cry I just roll over and carry on sleeping. Ironically, whilst this response was never meant to be taken seriously, it does in fact come a bit too close to the truth. In fact, I find it incredibly difficult to rouse myself from a deep slumber, however loudly the baby is crying. It goes further. Either through laziness or through some mysterious physical condition, I believe that I have become largely immune to the nocturnal crying of a baby. Quite simply, baby could be screaming for minutes on end, and I would still fail to respond. On those occasions that I actually have awoken, I have, in a state of drowsiness, considered the options, and then allowed my wife to do the business.

I never intended to be selfish in these or any other circumstances. I suppose I just allowed myself to get away with my sleepiness too often. Angela never chided me for taking this approach. She was usually too tired to chastise me. So, the habit was never broken. In my defence, when baby awoke, it was usually in order to demand milk. Since the baby refused to have milk from a bottle, I considered myself to be superfluous to proceedings. Even this excuse was not fully justifiable, though, since I conveniently ignored the issue of nappy changing. I adopted the view that since Mummy had to wake up to feed the baby anyway, then she might as well also change the nappy. This would mean that only one of us would be disturbed. Strange, really, since in many other aspects I consider myself to be a Millennium man. Not quite a new man, perhaps, but nearly new.

I once discussed this difficulty with an uncle who had plenty of experience in this field himself, having fathered two of my cousins. I think I was looking for some magical cure to my apparent inability to help out a bit more during night-time. My uncle drew from his own experience in telling me how he had helped out much more the second time around. It sounded like he was advising me to make sure that I did not follow the same pattern. This seemed like useful advice at the time. Unfortunately, I subsequently managed to use this knowledge as an excuse for continuing to take a back seat when it came to sorting out our first child during the night. I persuaded myself that I was merely following the precedent as set out by my uncle, and thought that if ever I had a second child, then I would also surely help out more.

I also talked the matter over with the secretary of my cricket club, who is a father of three. I discovered that he had been even worse than me when it came to answering the baby's cry. This fellow admitted that he would, on occasions, hear the crying, deliberately give his wife a nudge to wake her up, and then pretend to be asleep. He thus allowed himself to feel that he had actually responded in the interests of the baby, and still managed to continue in a pleasant state of slumber.

It is often suggested that if only one parent goes out to work, then that parent should be excused from nocturnal duties during the week. The payback is that the working parent should then take on the responsibilities at weekends. This sounds fine in theory, but looking after babies is never best suited by theories. I am no more able to suddenly snap out of my sleep on a Friday or a Saturday than I am on any other night during the week. If baby has to wait for me to realize what day of the week it is, he will be waiting and crying, a long time.

Guilt and Making Amends

Overall, I remember feeling an incredible sense of guilt for allowing Angela to take on so much of the nocturnal workload. I still maintain that it was reasonable for her to be in sole charge of breast-feeding, but I cannot help but feel that I could have contributed more in the areas of waste disposal and rocking baby back to sleep. Since the arrival of our second baby, I have been determined to try harder. I still find it difficult to respond to crying, but I no longer feel quite so justified in simply rolling over. At the very least, I think it helps that I now make an attempt to wake up and watch the nappy being changed, since this must offer a degree of moral support. Moreover, I have explained to Angela that I will now help out as long as she does all she can to ensure that I actually wake up. Perhaps I was mean not to explain this to her the first time round. Perhaps she will again be utterly selfless, and continue to allow me to sleep on in semi-ignorance. Still, at least I have given her the solution!

Three In a Bed

Any self-respecting child psychotherapist will discourage the habit of allowing baby to sleep in bed with the parents. The main reason for this is that baby will find it much harder to get used to sleeping alone in a cot later on. This, again, sounds fine in theory. In practice, the benefits from having the baby in the bed may well outweigh the disadvantages to be incurred later on. Nowadays, it often seems both practical and reasonable to allow baby to share the parental bed. Some parents even consider it a virtue to encourage such sleeping arrangements. At a recent wedding, one couple stated that they found the practice such a delight that they had just placed an order for a king-size bed, to provide more room for planned future arrivals.

One immediate benefit comes in not having to fetch the baby from the cot every time he wakes up for a feed. The immediate proximity of mother and baby reduces the time it takes for baby to be put onto the breast. Milk is thereby provided much more quickly. Another benefit comes in the form of easily being able to monitor the baby's temperature. If you, yourself, are too warm or too cold in bed, then the baby will feel the effect even more. Moreover, if the baby stills cries, despite being in such a favourable lie, then a quick cuddle will usually do the trick. The overall effect of these benefits is to minimize the likelihood of Daddy being disturbed unnecessarily, and that can only be good for all parties involved.

A big drawback to having baby in the bed is that you never really feel comfortable enough to go into a deep sleep. Mothers tend to sleep curled up around their babies, and this closeness is enough to disturb the sleep of both parties. Even when baby is positioned away from the mother – as far as space allows – baby always manages to go sleep-crawling in order to resume physical contact with Mummy. This kind of tropic movement does not, strangely, seem to involve the father, unless, of course, the mother is not present.

A more serious concern is the constant nagging thought that the tiny little being could be smothered or squashed. However rarely this happens, it is always a possibility, and the fear of it prevents parents from having a normal, fully refreshing sleep. Given the seriousness of this worry, light, broken sleep might be considered advantageous, since it allows regular check-ups on the baby's comfort and position. (The alternative view is that Mummy and Daddy would be less likely to roll over if they were in a much deeper sleep.)

To sum up, do not be misled into thinking that having the baby in the bed is necessarily the easy option. In some ways, it might be easier to leave the baby in the cot and allow him to cry himself to sleep – especially if you have the knack of shutting out the sound of crying.

A Room of One's Own

If the baby is not already sleeping on his own in a cot, the time will come, sooner or later, for him to have a room of his own. Conventional advice will already have suggested that this should take place as early as possible, but for reasons already explained, 'as early as possible' means different things to different families. In our case, the decision to make our first child sleep on her own was only really enforced by the happy news of a second pregnancy. There is nothing quite like pregnancy for focusing the mind. Allowing Georgina to spend her nights with us was clearly no longer an option. Not only was it already time to bestow upon her some degree of independence, it would also have been far too tiring for all of us.

The decision to break the habit of a baby's lifetime has to be followed up with a great deal of dedicated perseverance. In our case, the transition was made relatively easily, since the brunt of the disturbance was borne by Georgina's grandmother. I cannot emphasize enough the value of grandmothers in such matters. We were fortunate indeed to have someone who was prepared to help our little one through a most difficult stage. Amazingly enough, the level of crying was kept to a minimum. I had assumed that we would all have to suffer hitherto uncharted levels of noise, yet in the end, we scarcely heard a murmur. There are so many reasons to pay tribute to my mother-in-law, but I think I valued her assistance in this matter more than at any other time. She made a potentially woeful job seem very easy.

Developing Patterns of Sleep

Any self-respecting baby will lay down a series of laws when it comes to going to sleep, including the following:

1) Every attempt must be made to stay awake.
2) Crying is the best means of objecting to the inevitable.
3) The last cry is the loudest.
4) By a baby's finally agreeing to go to sleep, the parents are being granted a special favour.
5) The sleeping baby will naturally look extremely cute. The baby will know this, and will sleep happily in the knowledge that admiring glances will be forthcoming from all who are privileged to witness such a delicate vision of cuteness.
6) A warm and cosy environment is a fundamental requirement for sound sleeping. Expecting a baby to sleep in a cold room, or in a cold cot, is quite ridiculous, and will prolong the difficulties no end.

Resistance Is Futile

Whilst it may be difficult to persuade a baby to go to sleep, the baby must at some stage concede that sleep is inescapable. This concession may be made right from the outset, although it will not necessarily mean that sleep will be immediate. A few hours may even elapse before sleep finally arrives. Usually, anything up to an hour can be considered reasonable. In extreme cases of good fortune, the process may only take a few seconds. However long it takes, there is always an inevitability about having to fall asleep. Babies cannot be expected to give in to this inevitability, of course, and their refusal to acknowledge that resistance is futile will cause a great deal of frustration on the part of the parents.

An Eye-contact Sport

Above all things, the accompanying adult will not be allowed to leave the room until sleep has well and truly been engaged. The baby will do its utmost to keep the tiniest chink of an eye open, right up until the very last moment when true sleep finally arrives. Even when the eyes are totally closed, a baby that is still awake will continue to exercise incredibly perceptive sensory powers, and will immediately be aware of the premature departure of the compulsory companion.

Manoeuvring for Maximum Comfort

No one stays completely still during sleep. Babies seem to move around more than any other age group. For some reason, even pointing in the same direction all night is out of the question. Every angle must be experimented with, along with every possible variation in the level of covering. You could almost surmise that the process of going to sleep is regarded by the baby as a mini adventure course that must be completed before finally succumbing to a deep slumber. Even within a deep sleep, babies are still liable to shift around. Such tossing and turning is one key reason why babies really ought to be on their own.

As time goes by, and the toddling stage is reached, toddlers who refuse to put up with the constraints of a cot will demand the wider freedom of a bed. They will need an inordinate amount of freedom to express themselves, and the confining space of the cot will simply no longer prove acceptable. Twisting and turning will then become much more enjoyable and will play a significant part in the winding-down process. Beds are, of course, far easier to escape from than cots, although even cots may not keep the really adventurous penned in. As a precautionary measure, it is worthwhile placing pillows around the base of the cot. This will soften the landing of any daring type who makes it over the top. As a further measure, stair gates and night lights should be installed as soon as the child shows any signs of attempting an unauthorized nocturnal escapade, if not sooner.

Cuteness Revisited

If sleeping babies look cute, then sleeping toddlers look even cuter. Toddlers soon learn to devise variations on the basic foetal position, and will adopt a whole range of new poses during their periods of rest. This repertoire of positions automatically leads on from the increasingly expansive contortions. The most engaging night-time vision that I regularly witness is the image of my toddler lying on her back, with her hands placed delicately behind her head. In this position, Georgina is clearly at peace and in harmony with her own nocturnal world. One can but imagine that she is dreaming of beautiful things: of fluffy lambs, of mermaids, of fairy castles in the sky, and of the freedom to enjoy chunk after chunk of the chocolate that is forbidden to her during waking hours.

21

CHANGING TASTES

Hitting the Bottle

Discontinuing the practice of breastfeeding was as important as moving our baby out of the parental bed. Within the context of changing sleeping quarters, and sleeping partners, this process was fairly straightforward. Again, this was a pleasant surprise. Whilst breast milk was, for a limited extended period, still available during the daytime, it was plainly off the menu during the night-time. Georgina took this in her stride, and soon graduated to the entirely different formula feed.

Do not be misled into thinking that drinking formula milk is the same as drinking breast milk. Even if the contents were the same, and they are not, the experience of sucking from a rubber teat is hugely different from being in contact with the natural source. Nevertheless, Georgina showed a great deal of co-operation in accepting this dramatic change in her mode of feeding. This seemed to show an unselfishness well beyond her years; but then, all babies have to come to terms with this. Some, sadly, never even get the chance to sample the delights of home-produced milk.

Solid Beginnings

Four months is generally recognized as about the right time to start weaning a baby. At this stage, breast milk seemed to be the only thing that would really settle Georgina, and apart from the fact that night-time feeding was being phased out, we still could not see how to persuade Georgina to try something different for a change. Once you get stuck in a routine, it can be very difficult to break out of it. On the face of it, babies seem quite happy to carry on in the same time-honoured fashion. However, it is possible to underestimate a baby's levels of understanding and perception. Sometimes, babies can steal a march on their parents by recognizing an important landmark in their own development. Whether or not they let on to their parents is another matter.

We were helped in this matter, once again, by Georgina's grandmother. One day, without prompting, she decided that it was about time to cook a batch of carrot and parsnip to be mashed up for our four-month-old little milk guzzler. I am convinced that Georgina, herself, realized that it was time for something new, since she took to the vegetable puree with gusto. To an adult, a bowl of tepid, unseasoned, squashed mixed vegetables may seem rather undesirable. To a baby, with far more sensitive taste buds, it can seem like a dish fit for the gods.

Processed Food

Having given Georgina such a wholesome start, she plainly acquired a taste for home cooking. This was so much the case that she subsequently turned down anything that came out of a jar or a packet. Her reactions to such foodstuffs were extreme. On the rare occasions that she would condescend to eat processed food, she would bring it back up with alacrity. Even so-called organic food was rejected. All this was ironic in that one of Georgina's aunts had, as a baby, won the 'Jamaica's Bonniest Baby' competition, as sponsored by Cow and Gate. Jamaica's bonniest baby never actually ate Cow and Gate food, but was happy to wear the Cow and Gate crown. Georgina, in contrast, wanted no association whatsoever with the commercial food industry.

An Expanding Palate

We very quickly came to settle on a menu that was based purely on simple, home-prepared dishes. For breakfast, lunch, and dinner, Georgina would eat any selection from the following:

cornmeal porridge; oat porridge; rice pudding;
pureed apples, pears, and prunes;
mashed carrots, parsnips, and swedes.

As the recipes became more advanced, one vital ingredient came to the fore: garlic. Garlic came to be included in almost every savoury dish on offer. Not just cloves of garlic, but copious, pungent amounts of garlic. On occasions, it seemed like whole strings of garlic found their way into the pot. Well, no self-respecting grandmother with a keen eye on Nature's rich bounty of medicinal plants was going to forget this wonder bulb. Perhaps the packet foods just did not include any garlic.

Biting Points

Before long, chicken was added to the menu. Even though no teeth were to arrive until after a year, quality pieces of chicken breast were gladly devoured. Instead of teeth, the gums did all the chewing; and what a powerful set of gums they were. The strength of gums had somehow been known about by my wife all along. It was only really impressed upon me now, as I saw the morsels of chicken disappear so rapidly, and subsequently when I dared to venture a little finger inside Georgina's mouth, in search of teeth. I soon learnt that the risk involved in doing this was almost Herculean, and decided that it did not really matter how quickly the teeth arrived. It was far better to make a ritual sacrifice out of a breadstick than a finger.

111

Concessions

As time went by, Georgina made two concessions towards processed wares. First, she came to develop a taste for soya-based yoghurts, but only those brands that did not include added sugar. Second, she happily accepted baby fruit juices, making no distinction between recognized brands and own-label products. Anything more substantial than this would either cause a puffed-up face or a round of puking; both, in some cases. Looking at the lists of ingredients, particularly on the organically grown and processed items, it seems a bit strange that Georgina dismissed them so summarily. The only conclusion that we could come to was that she had already developed a strong sense of how to do things properly in life, and would accept nothing less.

Fortunately, Angela was happy to oblige in devoting herself to preparing hearty, wholesome meals. On most occasions, cooking for our baby was almost a privilege, rather than a chore. Sometimes, though, mashing up vegetables and pushing them through a sieve did cause a certain amount of ennui. On one particularly vexing occasion, a complete batch of carrots, broccoli, and courgettes had to be thrown away after the tip of a knife snapped off and disappeared without trace within the pulp. Preparing a second batch was quite trying, but then, nothing is too much trouble for baby.

Chips with Everything

For the first sixteen months of Georgina's life, we were happy with the kind of food and drink that made up her diet. If anything, we were perhaps a little smug at the wholesome quality of her intake. Good things rarely last forever. Changes began to happen whilst on holiday in Jamaica. Whilst the Wyndham Rose Hall is one of the finest hotels that Montego Bay can offer, it does not lend itself particularly well to the dietary requirements of a growing baby.

112

It was at the Wyndham that Georgina had her first ever taste of chips. This seemed a good idea at the time, since little else suitable jumped off the poolside grill bar menu. There I was, expecting Georgina to turn her nose up at this newly proffered dish, and blow me down if she didn't scoff the lot! We were all astonished to see her tucking in heartily to what previously had been not just forbidden, but also unsolicited food. Well, following on from this rather dubious success, chips became almost a daily habit during our stay in Jamaica.

Back home, I feel happier providing Georgina with home-made chips, since at least I can guarantee the quality of the potatoes and the cooking oil. Thankfully, after a spell during which our innocent, wholesome little girl repeatedly announced her favourite meal to be 'MILK AND CHIPS', her interest in chips seems to be on the wane. The downside to this minor improvement is that chips are now used merely as a means of obtaining tomato ketchup. Additionally, a strong predilection is now being exhibited for Mini Cheddars, crisps, and Hula Hoops, or 'Hulan Hoops', as Georgina so cutely calls them. At least all these items provide a valuable source of carbohydrates, and in this respect, Georgina is simply taking after her father. I have always placed great faith in carbohydrates.

Sweet Tooth

The growing taste for fried carbohydrates has run in parallel to an increased desire for chocolate. I think it fair to say, even, that Georgina's appetite for chocolate is matched only by that of Deanna Troi, the Counsellor on board the *Enterprise*. Now, this liking for chocolate is something of a mystery to us. Nobody ever advised our child that chocolate was an exciting food to eat. Nobody, certainly, suggested that it was a food to crave after. Somewhere along the line, Georgina must have discovered for herself that chocolate was out of this world. The speed with which she attacks a box of Tesco's finest truffles that has fallen onto the floor is something to behold. Having secured possession of one of the said truffles, it is very nearly an impossible task to remove it from her grasp. Chances are, she will already have shoved it into her dainty little mouth by the time it takes to attempt a recovery operation.

Strangely enough, no other items of confectionery have ever had the same effect. On many occasions, the friendly owners of a nearby corner shop have offered sweeties, and whilst we have tended to discourage this practice, Georgina has never really complained about being denied any treats. Now, if the word 'chocolate' were to be mentioned, then we would either have to allow the gift or leave the shop with one extremely unhappy, screaming child.

To sum up, however good one's intentions are, there will be times when adapting to circumstances and adopting a more liberal approach will seem like a perfectly reasonable course of action.

22

ROOM FOR MANOEUVRE

Adapting to a new environment is a challenge that has to be met by both adults and children alike.

For the child, having surmounted the hardship of leaving the comforts of the womb and entering the outside world, there is now a less dramatic, but significant problem to face up to. This is the challenge of finding a niche in life, of finding a place within the family home. This may simply involve taking possession of a nursery, and later on, a bedroom. It may otherwise mean claiming a space within Mummy and Daddy's bedroom, or in the inner sanctum of a sibling's room. In addition to sleeping quarters, a child will have to discover those areas in the house and garden that are accessible, and those that are out of bounds and hence liable to result in a ticking off for stepping out of line.

The nature of the challenge will be different depending on whether or not there are any older brothers or sisters. A first child will be the first in the family to have to carve out a place for himself within a previously adult-only environment. For subsequent children, the rite of passage will be easier, since the parents will be experienced in the art of making children welcome, but still, there will be difficulties to overcome. In this instance, subsequent children will have to invade the space of the previous child. This might not always be a totally harmonious affair.

As children come into the household, and as they grow bigger, parents also have to learn to accommodate the developing needs of their cherished offspring. This means not just loving each child with hugs and kisses, but also providing a very real space which the child can learn to grow into and move within. This will usually mean giving over a part, or parts of the house which were previously solely inhabited by adults. As time goes by, all areas in the house will become fair game, and Mummy and Daddy will no longer have space of their own. Providing space for children does not simply mean buying a house with a bedroom for each child. It means, on a wider scale, welcoming other people into your own little kingdom, an area that was once enjoyed solely by a childless couple.

Space, of course, is not the end of it. What goes on within that space is the next big issue. Sharing a living space with children means not always being able to watch the test match live on television. This may well be curtailed by the need to allow *Bob the Builder* or the *Tweenies* onto the screen, no matter how many times the same videos have been watched previously. It also means allowing the house to become cluttered with toys. Children's toys have a habit of coming in many small pieces that must be strewn across the room in order to provide satisfactory entertainment for the children. Finally, it also means having to look out for little ones under your feet. It is extremely easy not to know exactly where a small child is in the room. Tiny children like to stand silently behind or adjacent to their parents. When this happens, an adult may tread on a child, or knock a child out of the way, simply by turning round.

Beginnings of Toddling

By the time that our first toddler was about a year old, she had already mastered the art of self-propulsion. The way that she moved around on the floor involved striding forward with one leg, whilst dragging the other leg behind, and this proved to be highly amusing to all who saw her doing so. Not really a crawl, not quite a walk, but something in between. Numerous babies of a similar age and disposition all tried and failed to mimic what seemed to be an inimitable mode of travel. Those who came close to the style could not match the pace, for Georgina was, indeed, faster than a galaxy-class starship.

Penned In

In an attempt to limit Georgina's field of play, we came up with the idea of a playpen. Some friends advised against such an idea, suggesting that such a restriction would not really work. We still considered that a playpen might help us out, and we then had the chance to try out the theory when we were permanently lent a playpen. Just as had been predicted, the pen was not a success. Initially, Georgina would play the game, on condition that she was provided with a plenitude of suitable toys. However, the extent of her tolerance level was approximately five minutes. After this time, Georgina would object to being left in what must have seemed like a trap, and would demand to be released.

Sometimes, these five minutes were enough to allow us to perform useful tasks. Usually, the benefits were outweighed by the frustration. After a while, we decided to abandon the playpen, and used it instead as a barricade, to prevent access to the computer cables under the desk in the corner of the sitting room. Once again, we learnt that you cannot keep a good toddler down.

23

PICKING THINGS UP

The term 'growing up' applies not just to developing children, but also to parents. Parents do, after all, have to grow into their new position, assuming all the cares and responsibilities previously outside their domain. Along with all the joys and excitement of parenthood, a parent will sooner or later have to come to terms with an ever-changing lifestyle. You may try to believe that having a baby will not change your ways, but really this is inconceivable.

Apart from the major changes involving having children, there will be a host of little things that steadily cause a change in attitude and behaviour, particularly in relation to possessions. Long before I had considered having my own children, I had been surprised and slightly annoyed to see young nephews and nieces rampaging throughout our house, picking up whatever objects took their fancy, mistreating them, and laying them down in totally unsuitable locations. I remember thinking at the time that this sort of behaviour was quite unacceptable, and that their parents should simply instruct their children to behave better. My sister was quick to point out that with children, things are never that simple. She informed me that attitudes towards possessions change when you become a parent. 'You'll be amazed,' I was told, 'at the things you allow your child to do. Possessions just become less important.'

Many of these changes will not become apparent until the baby has become a toddler, or has at least learnt how to move around without being carried. It is advisable, from time to time, to step back and to consider how you react to seeing your cute little toddler viciously ripping up valuable documents, or tearing out pages from expensive books. The books don't even have to be classic tales. It can be highly vexing even to come across a copy of *Dotty Dog Goes to the Seaside*, only to realize that all the action on the beach is described on pages that have long since been torn out, screwed up, eaten, or all three. It feels worse still when the child graduates from his own story books to Mummy and Daddy's books.

Despite the obvious signs of danger, you never really expect a toddler to want to handle your own, more adult works of literature. Never underestimate a child's determination to explore. Put another way, there are no bounds to a child's desire to be mischievous. I have learnt this at close hand, having watched Georgina climb up onto the arm of the sofa, in order to reach the cricketing tomes on the top shelf of the bookcase in the sitting room. I have discouraged this line of enquiry, on two counts. First, I do not wish to see her fall off the sofa and hurt herself. Secondly, I do not wish to see any of my books mistreated. I hope I have my priorities right, here.

Not only is a child determined to be mischievous, a child is determined to be so repeatedly. The incident on the sofa was not an isolated occurrence. I am sure that Georgina has enjoyed many escapades of this nature. I have evidence of this, in the form of a chewed spine on my copy of *The Book of Cricket Lists*, and of a torn cover on my *Second Golden Age of Cricket*.

Letting Go for a Reason

Subconsciously, perhaps, adults allow children increasing levels of access to things that should not be touched, in order to observe how well-behaved their children have become. I live in daily dread of seeing my prized collection of beautifully bound *Wisden Cricket Monthlies* wrenched from the bookshelf and vandalized indiscriminately. Yet, because I want to believe that Georgina is learning to exercise some discretion, and because I have not yet witnessed a specific attempt at such an outrage, I have not seen fit to remove the works to a place of safety.

Foolishly, perhaps, I am giving Georgina the chance to prove that she can recognize how dearly her Daddy cherishes those chocolate-coloured binders; and she is not yet two years old! It will all end in tears, I am sure, but perhaps, by then, my tolerance level will have increased sufficiently to forgive her for committing such treachery. Perhaps – and I realize that I keep using the word 'perhaps', since one of the wonders of bringing up a family is that you never know exactly how things will work out – perhaps I will not seek to punish Georgina for tearing up my *Wisdens*, because I will have come to appreciate that there are far more important things in life than a set of magazines. Never mind the fact that I have collected them religiously over the last eleven years, have read them all cover to cover, and have set myself the task of preserving them for as long as I have my wits about me. Never mind all this? Let's hope I can come round to this point of view, should I ever need to.

Lack of Challenge?

Angela has suggested that Georgina keeps her hands off my *Wisdens* simply *because* they are in reach, and that such easy access hardly represents a challenge to a highly resourceful young mischief-maker. I could go along with this, were it not for the fact that however many times I instruct Georgina to leave my collection of Clint Eastwood video cassettes alone, she returns to them with monotonous regularity. Many has been the time when I have come home, only to find that my precariously labelled videos have all been jumbled up, leaving me with the tedious task of trying to match up each stray post-it note to its rightful video.

A second example that argues against the 'ease of reach'

theory was provided by my experience with seed trays. Again, despite straightforward advice to the contrary, Georgina waited patiently for just the right opportunity to pull out a handful of Brussels sprout plants that I had carefully nurtured from seeds. A wanton act of destruction, if ever there was one, and the perpetrator remained totally oblivious to the significance of her malefaction.

A Woman's Hand

My wife undoubtedly sees many things differently. I have talked of the theory of keeping things in perspective, of placing more value on the child than on material goods, but my views are largely theoretical. Since I am out of the house from eight until six, Monday to Friday, Angela has much more experience of the reality of our child's mischief.

On seeing varying degrees of damage to supposedly important objects, I have, at times, unfairly criticized Angela for allowing Georgina to have too free a run of the house. I know this is unfair because, if anything, she spends more time trying to look after my possessions than her own. This, she does, through being unselfish, and from not wanting to see me become grumpy. At times, I have even suggested that I am the only one who cares about the risk of a piece of toast being inserted into the video cassette recorder. This suggestion is nonsense. Of course Angela does not want to watch repeated images of a browned-off slice of Hovis any more than I do. The reality is that she is a) unable to keep an eye on our little one all the time; b) too tired to be constantly following the little scamp wherever she goes; and c) unwilling to restrict our child's development in such an absolute fashion.

Children do, after all, need constantly to be allowed to experiment and to learn to perform new activities. The knock-on effect of this is that material goods may well take a knock along the way. Food may be thrown all over the carpet, ornaments may be broken, and wallpaper may be covered in crayon markings. Such accidents and misdemeanours are inevitable. There is no satisfactory way of allowing a child to grow up without making what we, as adults, perceive to be mistakes. At such a young age, trying to stop a toddler from learning is simply unreasonable. You might as well try to stop toddlers from toddling altogether.

Feminine Generosity

Women, in general, are less selfish than men. After all, they are forced into this position by the very nature of pregnancy. Women have to give up so much more of their bodies, and of their time, and probably of their emotions too, than their male counterparts. It follows on, then, that mothers will become kinder and more generous to their offspring, in terms of what they allow their children to get up to, and in the more meaningful gifts of generosity. Fathers may give more presents to their children, but that could well be because in many cases it is the father who keeps control of the purse strings, and who is in more of a position to blow away the family income on fripperies. Mothers, on the other hand, have a greater need to work within a limited budget. The old concept of housekeeping money springs to mind, although this will undoubtedly raise the hackles of all those mothers who work and may even earn more than their partners. Still, even though the mothers are likely to have fewer financial resources than the fathers, mothers still manage to be incredibly resourceful when it comes to providing for their young. More often than not, mothers will sacrifice their own goods or entitlements in order to enrich the lives of their children.

A simple example of this, but one which has always stuck in the memory is how my own mother always used to share her chocolate bars. Despite the fact that I and my three siblings regularly used to receive a veritable bounty of confectionery items from a generous grandmother, we always ended up being offered a share of our mother's solitary chocolate bar, long after our own rich supplies had been devoured. I can remember making a half-hearted attempt to refuse this kind offer, on the grounds that the chocolate belonged to her, that we did not deserve it, and that Mother was just not being fair to herself. The response was always the same: 'Yes, it is mine, but I choose to let you all have some of it.' Well, a Mars bar shared six ways does not go a long way, but it was the gesture that counted, and it came from the heart.

24

SMACKS OF DISCIPLINE

There is a time, of course, when certain actions need to be prevented or discontinued. When a piece of mischief is deemed serious enough, you simply have to deploy some form of discipline. My main area of concern here is that of physical discipline, and the issue of smacking naughty children. Despite all the attempts of Greater Europe to standardize the acceptable methods of discipline, such measures should, and do, remain the responsibility of the family. Guidelines may be suggested, but no amount of edicts from Brussels can take the place of a good bit of parental discretion.

Before we go any further, just in case you were worried, I must state that I am not including babies in the category of children that might give cause to be deemed naughty. Babies, as far as I am concerned, are blemish free. One of the joys of looking at a baby comes in the appreciation of a little human being that has never done anything wrong in his entire life. The innocence of babies is a marvellous thing. Babies, of course, should never be struck. Heaven forbid.

You may wonder, at this point, how even a toddler could do anything that could possibly justify a smack. Well, up to a certain stage, I would say that toddlers also enjoy a privileged status, and thus qualify for exeption from corporal punishment. There will come a stage, however, when a toddler voluntarily relinquishes the condition of angelic perfection. Sooner or later, a child is almost duty bound to drive his parents up the wall with various misdeeds and misbehaviour. That is all part of growing up. The downside to this development is that it needs to be controlled.

My views on the best means of control have changed drastically within the last two years. I used to believe that smacking was an inescapable feature of family life. I went further than this, even, in arguing that smacking was a valuable and necessary tool in the administration of discipline, albeit a tool that you should never enjoy using, and one that should never be used in excess. Even now, I still have lingering thoughts that smacking is valid and effective under specific circumstances, and cannot simply be abolished.

Whether smacking is effective or not depends on a number of key factors. Of most importance, I would argue, is the level of understanding involved by both the punished and the punisher. It is simply wrong to punish a child without making sure that the child knows why the punishment is being administered. In all cases the ability to appreciate how much is being understood is paramount. The misbehaving child must know why a smack is being delivered. It should also be obvious that the punishment is relevant to a particular act of naughtiness. General misbehaviour is not a justification for specific punishment. Similarly, it is wrong to punish a child without fully realizing why you are doing it. The biggest mistake an adult can make, here, is the mistake of being out of control, and of acting inexplicably out of character.

The effectiveness of smacking is also dependent on the degree of force applied, the frequency of its application, and the target area for the hitting. From my own experience, some of which I now regret, I believe I always deployed what seemed at the time to be the appropriate strength in my smacking. Tears nearly always resulted from my smacks, but usually, they were crocodile tears, and always short-lived. I tended to regard these pretensions of hurt as an appropriate recognition of guilt, and as a sign of a wanting to show due penitence, if only on a very outward and shallow level.

I really don't think I have to be *too* hard on myself, because on the rare occasions when Georgina has transgressed, the force of the resulting corrective measures was minimal, and always applied to the thickly padded area protected by one of Pampers' finest. I used to find even this mild gesture of disapproval hard to perform in earnest, and I often immediately followed up the pat on the behind with a loving kiss. Sometimes, the smack and the kiss might even have seemed simultaneous. This was never intended, and was almost certainly confusing. It just illustrates the importance of everybody understanding what is going on. Surely it would be too much to believe that Georgina recognized, on those highly charged occasions, that the smacking was both necessary and regrettable at the same time. Devon, of course, has been exempt from all this.

I am trying to make it sound as if smacking is totally a thing of the past in my family. I wish! What I can say is that it is now extremely rare. For the moment, simply mentioning the word 'smack' is enough to stop the mischief. Using this kind of threat is wrong in itself, but becoming a totally reformed character does not happen over night. Besides, I do not think this practice will last, since empty threats soon lose their power. In preparation for this, I am currently working on alternative methods for restoring order when juvenile transgressions challenge the desired state of harmony.

The main reason for my conviction? Having seen little children hit each other, I came to realize that you cannot expect to set them a good example if *you* employ any sort of violence towards *them* whatsoever. As adults, we know that smacking a naughty child is vastly different from that same child bashing a playmate over the head with a toy brick, but children cannot recognize the difference. As parents, we are the ultimate role models, and we must behave in a manner that we are happy to see copied. If we smack our children, and they decide to smack us back, where will it end?

In an ideal world, the need – or perhaps the opportunity

– for punishment would be reduced, in many cases, if the parents had more time to spend with their children. It may seem acceptable, for example, to take objects away from a child, and to punish that child for naughtily taking it back again, but it would be so much better to provide a suitable alternative to play with. It would be easy, again, to punish a child for pulling up the flowers in the garden, but it would be far more constructive to do some basic gardening together. These are fairly trivial things. Preventing more serious misdeeds will require more thought. As a general rule, by being more available for your children, they will have less chance to become bored and will not be so easily tempted to behave mischievously.

Despite all the best intentions in the world, if smacking has to be performed – for whatever the reason – it must be done with obvious regret, rather than with anger. Furthermore, it is quite simply unacceptable to let it become part of a routine. As with so many aspects of life, finding the right way to do things is not always easy. Learning to be uncomfortable with smacking is a good place to start when it comes to discovering how best to react to wrongdoing.

25

BITING ONE'S TONGUE

Within any relationship, there is always a potential for conflict. For new and developing parents, there will be an abundance of new situations presenting tests of character and other significant challenges. Babies and toddlers that simply do as they have been known to do throughout history find both new and repeated ways of driving you up the wall on a daily basis. Knowing in advance that trying times are on the way does not really make things easier when the causes of frustration actually arise. Emotions run high, blame is easily apportioned, and tolerance is stretched to the limit. At this stage in life, the scope for differences of opinion is massive. The chances of a problem-free relationship are extremely remote. Overcoming such wide-ranging difficulties usually proves more complicated than it should be, and, as a result, there is a much greater likelihood of exchanging unpleasantries.

In some ways, heated disagreement can be a valuable way of working towards a better understanding. You never quite know exactly what your partner is thinking, or why, and it is important to keep hailing frequencies open constantly. Often, issues do not become resolved until they have been fully aired and disputed. Hence, communication is paramount. The danger is that even the slightest criticism can result in a full-blown argument. Trifling concerns so easily become serious disputes that are generally misguided and subsequently regretted.

It does not take much experience in this area to realize that an easy way to start an argument is to point out a minor peccadillo on the part of your partner. The intention may be to get something off your chest, or to justify yourself, or to apportion blame for a perceived oversight. Whatever the reason, the injured party will immediately feel picked on, particularly if the tone of voice is lacking in any warmth, affection, and humour. The situation will be exacerbated if one or both partners is tired. This is the worst time to argue. Under such conditions, a few unnecessary and hurtful words will quickly develop into a cross and mean-spirited exchange of views. If left unresolved, and repeat performances ensue, the originally petty motives for starting a squabble may develop into a constant desire to be antagonistic.

All too often, minor differences of opinion are expressed through cutting remarks and unreasonable accusations. Bear in mind that a tense situation is not likely to be quickly resolved by allowing yourself to appear to be a disgruntled, inconsiderate brute with nothing pleasant to say. Caustic, chiding comments are never called for, and rarely – if ever – produce the kind of reaction that you should be hoping for. You may feel some smug satisfaction at being able to provoke a hostile response, but, deep down, it does not really feel good to bring the worst out in someone else. Certainly not if that person is the loving mother of one's child. There may be every excuse, but no justification for being nasty to a loved one.

Having said all this, I do not claim to have the secret to holding one's tongue. The temptation to have a little dig can prove almost irresistible. I merely offer the following reflection:

Sarcasm is not only the lowest form of wit; it is also the form of wit most likely to cause offence and to start an argument. Before coming out with something smart that makes you feel better for an instant, consider the far more rewarding happiness that would result from a gentle approach and a few kind words. Strive to acquire the patience of Job.

26

PULLING ONE'S WEIGHT

Humans seldom respond well, initially, to lifestyle changes that take place suddenly, or to changes that are caused by events outside of our control. Even when we are the cause of our own changing circumstances, it can take a while to come to terms with them. For new mothers, adapting to change is a matter of immediate necessity. They have virtually no chance to forget their responsibilities, and are generally very good at fulfilling them. For new fathers, it should be possible to say the same, but I suspect that this is not quite so. I suggest that many men like to feel that they still have some sort of choice about how to lead their lives, and, more specifically, how much they want to be involved with the new baby. In this light, consider the following alternatives as models for the developing father.

1. Mr. Take-It-Easy

Where the opportunity arises, Mr. Take-It-Easy succumbs to the temptation of taking a back seat. He allows, and comes to expect the mother to take on a rather more substantial share of the workload than might be considered absolutely fair: say ninety per cent. Sooner or later, the mother will begin to cotton on, and will start dropping hints relating to the disparity between their respective shares of the chores. Realizing that the mother feels overworked, the father has the chance to redress the balance by making more of an effort. But no, Mr. Take-It-Easy then tries to make his wife feel guilty for behaving irritably. This is easily done by talking to her about communication, understanding and unselfishness. Still, knowing that his lifestyle of complacency is under threat, Mr. Take-It-Easy then decides to start trying to make the baby behave more reasonably. After all, if the mother is not prepared to do it all, then surely baby should be encouraged to fend for himself a bit more. Of course, Mr. Take-It-Easy will not accept that the baby does not enjoy lying in a pram for hours on end, with only a rattle and a cuddly teddy for amusement. Baby's demands to be picked up fall on deaf ears, and would otherwise be regarded as something of an imposition.

Leaning on a partner may be acceptable some of the time, and may even be welcomed within the right context. But, coming home from work and assuming that dinner is only ten minutes away is asking a bit much. Walking through the door and expecting to find a tidy house is not reasonable. Preparing to relax after a hard day's work shows an all-round lack of consideration. To crown it all, asking, even thinking the question 'What *have* you been doing all day?' is the surest way to upset one's wife.

Allowing the mother to believe that she is responsible for always stopping the crying and the mischief, and everything else that goes on in the house, is simply unkind. Making her feel inadequate, or even worse, lazy, will never do any good.

2. Mr. Dynamic

Either through free will, or due to an initial element of prodding, Mr. Dynamic relishes the opportunity to spend time alone with his baby. Recognizing that this is the new Millennium, and keen not to have to admit to friends and family that he is having an easy time of it, Mr. Dynamic does everything possible to help bring up the baby. This includes changing nappies regularly, not just once a week; bathing the baby; dressing the baby; pushing the pram out for walks in the park; and, generally, taking his turn at assuming complete responsibility for the baby. On these occasions, the father must be alone with the child, since a hovering mother always deters the father from taking complete responsibility. Should the mother be present, not only will the father feel hesitant to make decisions for himself, but the baby, also, will feel the need to summon Mummy for a cuddle or a helping of breast. By spending genuine one-on-one time in this way, Mr. Dynamic not only enjoys frequent bonding sessions with his baby, he also becomes proficient in all aspects of baby care. It follows on that Mrs. Dynamic is then free to pursue non-baby-related interests.

The value of having time to think straight and to relax is inestimable for the mother. Furthermore, by showing a willingness to be involved with, and to take responsibility for the child, the father is also restating his commitment to the mother. This allows each member of the family to feel confident and at ease with each other. Happiness will abound within the home.

This all sounds so good in theory. I must remember to try it sometime; maybe with next baby but one . . .

27

GETTING BACK IN THE SADDLE

As pointed out earlier in the book, sex is a highly personal matter, and I still do not intend to participate in any more than a nodding acquaintance with the topic. Nevertheless, picking up where you left off does warrant some consideration, so here goes . . .

Abstaining from sex is recommended for at least the first six weeks following the birth. Six weeks is the minimum; the period of abstinence could be considerably longer. I have even heard scare stories relating how one or both partners went off the idea altogether, as a result of being adversely affected by the experience of labour. Granted, the scenes in the delivery suite do not inspire any amorous designs at the time, but they rarely put you off for life.

During the enforced lay-off, it is more than likely that there will be a whole host of other activities guaranteed to take one's mind off the subject. All the extra chores and hassles will also lead to feeling just too tired to consider it. Once the option returns, the best plan of action is probably to relax, wait for one's partner to make the first move, and take things as they come. Precautions will be necessary, but this is not the end of the world. At some stage, you might, after all, feel like going through the whole rigmarole all over again. This will then allow another round of unprotected revelry.

Given that the baby in the nursery might wake up and demand attention at any moment, be prepared to cut down on the foreplay or to skip the after-match cigarette. Time will be at a premium.

28

TESTING TIMES

For parents, it is very easy to lose track of time, and to fail to recognize certain key moments in the early stages of a baby's development. If it were not for the regular weekly or fortnightly visits to the clinic and the monthly vaccinations in the first few months, then you could easily see your concept of time fly out of the window.

The little red book provided by the health authority helps in this matter, by presenting charts and questionnaires to help monitor every milestone in the baby's development. Not only is it fun to write down exactly how many weeks old baby was when he first smiled, or when he first laughed, or when he first tasted solids, but it also helps to add some kind of immediacy to the time frame of development. Babies grow up so quickly, and it is important to recognize the speed of growth in order to enjoy the baby at its smallest. Each stage in the development is exciting, but miss out on any stage, particularly the early ones, and you will subsequently feel disappointed at having failed to experience an event in life that will never be repeated.

Imagine getting up very late on the day of a test match, only to arrive at Edgbaston in time to be told that Phil De Freitas has already taken two wickets with the first two balls of the morning. Any number of screenings of the highlights later that evening could not really compensate for not actually witnessing the live action. In the same way, looking at photographs and videos of a baby growing up would simply not be the same as being there.

Consider how wasteful you would feel at missing out on

an experience, and on a rich source of happy memories, that was simply there for the taking. You have a responsibility to yourself to make the effort to be involved and to take an interest. This applies both to watching test matches and to participating in the bringing up of baby.

Failing to attend at the start of a cricket match is quite dreadful, in that it will cause all sorts of feelings of guilt, self-recrimination, and a deep sense of loss. Still, at least there will always be another day, another match. In the case of a growing baby, repeat performances may never be re-enacted in quite the same way. The only way to try and make up for such a loss would be to have another baby, and to be present for a similar event the next time round. The next time, it might be Dominic Cork taking a hat trick against the West Indies, and what a shame it would be to repeat the original mistake. Similarly, the second baby might just manage three shredded wheats for breakfast one day. Or, perhaps, he might, at a very early stage, call for Daddy to read him the story of *The Three Little Pigs*, having heard about it from baby number one. Maybe, even, baby number two might say the magic word 'Daddy' for the first time at nine months rather than twelve months. What a pity it would be to be absent on all or any of these occasions.

Having said this, both mother and father cannot always be there. In some ways, it would be a bad thing for all concerned if they were. This is fortunate, really, since someone has to go out to earn a crust.

Workable Alternatives

Current social trends tend to oblige mothers to go back to work after a period deemed sufficient to give baby a start in life. This appears to be the case regardless of whether or not the woman either wishes or needs to go back into the rat race.

It is not unusual for mothers of very young children to go out to work in order to pay for someone else to mind their

135

little treasures. As the children grow older, the money is then needed to pay for nursery education. In some cases the money earned is just enough for this sole purpose, and no more. The irony here, of course, is that if the mothers were not away from home all day, then they would not have to pay to send their children somewhere else. Under these specific circumstances, where there is nothing extra to be gained from both parents working, it makes sense to buck the trend. Still, writing this is making me feel frightfully old-fashioned.

I am fully aware that there are other reasons why a woman should want to return to work, including a genuine career interest, a preference for adult company, and a wish to exercise a 'right' not to be confined to domesticity. Should these, or any other reasons apply, then the mother and father should decide between them how best to organize the care of their children. Furthermore, I do not suggest that the emphasis should always be on the woman to justify her choice to work. I simply represent the situation as it appears to manifest itself within the context of our current sense of traditionalism.

Ideally, the best situation is for only one parent in the family to go out to work. This does not necessarily have to be the father, although I think this is preferable in the early stages of a baby's life. So far, this has worked out extremely well within my own family. Moreover, I think this works well for the nation, too. There are only so many jobs to go round, and if both parents in one family work, then the chances are that both parents in another family will be unemployed. A simplistic view, perhaps, but one that always impresses me.

When Angela was still pregnant, I proposed a straight-forward way of tackling the issue. I stated that during the early months, and probably the early years of our baby's development, at least one of his parents should be constantly on hand to attend to his every need. I made the concession that although I thought that this responsibility belonged to the mother, I might possibly consider taking on the role myself. The condition I attached to this concession was that Angela would have to be in a position to earn more than I did in my job. As it turned out, she was more than happy to forget all about her office life, since this had never really appealed to her anyway.

Much later on, in a conversation with a former colleague, I let on that I was glad that my wife had agreed not to return to work. My colleague suggested that I must be extremely generous to want to support my wife in this way, the implication being that life at home with a child was something of a doddle. Far from it. Now, as a mother within the home, she works at least as hard, and probably harder than many who work within a commercial environment. The same applies to most houseparents. Being the sole breadwinner does not necessarily mean being the most industrious member of the family.

In time, the situation may change, and Angela may decide that she would like to pursue some form of gainful employment outside the home, perhaps on a part-time basis. This is obviously an option, but for the time being, we are all content within our current positions.

The Nanny State

The alternative of the mother going back to work requires the provision of somebody else to act as a childminder or nanny to your beloved offspring. Now, even if the arrangement is financially beneficial, or desirable in some other way, you have to question the wisdom of allowing a total stranger to be the most dominant presence in baby's daily life. There is a possibility, of course, that the nanny might be a friend or a relative, and this could improve the situation significantly. But, wherever possible, and I acknowledge that in many cases it is not possible, a baby should have easy access to a loving parent or two.

First of all, I personally would not wish to run the risk of allowing any other person, with the obvious exception of my wife, to develop a closer relationship with my baby than I could myself. This might sound selfish, and perhaps it is, but I will not be dissuaded from believing that the two most important people in a baby's life should be the baby's mother and father.

Second, I am much more prepared to make cutbacks than to see Angela leave baby behind every day, merely to maintain our fairly affluent lifestyle. Material goods are important, and I would hate to have to deny my child anything. However, you cannot provide *everything* in this life, and it is important to establish an appreciation for those things in life that really are important. By this, I include such things as a mother smiling at her baby, laughing with her baby, holding her baby, feeding her baby, and playing with her baby. Substitute 'father' for 'mother' and 'his' for 'her' if you will, but the principle still holds good. Presence, rather than presents, is the key issue here. Any number of fancy toys or clothes from Baby Gap cannot compensate for the loss of personal contact.

I could be wrong, and I would be delighted to be proved thus, but the acceptance of nannies seems to be increasing in society. I recognize that my values are out of line with contemporary thought, but I will make short shrift of any advice in favour of sheepishly tagging along with the Nannites.

29

LEARNING AND COMMUNICATING

Reading

Reading is a fine way of spending time with your children.

If a father says that he does not have time to read to his children, then he simply does not have time for his children. Quite simply, reading is one of the fundamental activities involved in bringing up the next generation. It is important not only to the children in terms of educational development, but also to the parents, who will glean much joy from watching their children learn.

Reading can play another important role. A story at bedtime is a useful way to encourage children to sleep. Two stories will have an even better chance of causing drowsiness, and ten stories really should be enough for even the most insomniac of children. One thing to look out for is the way that children try to turn story time into an extension of the day's play, with no intention of entering the land of nod. Make it fun, of course, but insist on the fact that lying down for the night is the correct response to the spoken tale. Remember, also, that reading at night-time should be supplementary to, not instead of, time spent together during the child's waking hours.

There is always a danger, of course, that reading could be used as a means of avoiding any other form of meaningful contact with your children. As a form of talking, it can help to stimulate development, and it can encourage bonding. However, the activity involves speaking the words of someone else, and could be seen as a way of not really having to talk to each other.

One question remains: how old should a child be before reading commences? I do not think there is a minimum age. Basically, even if the tiniest of babies does not quite understand all the nuances of the Flopsy Bunnies, there is still a great deal of pleasure to be had from hearing Mummy or Daddy's voice. Open the first book as soon as you have the inclination.

Hailing Frequencies Open

Having listened to story after story, not to mention the everyday speech of adults and older children, the time will come for toddlers to open their mouths in order to do their own verbalizing. First words always bring great delight to parents. Fathers tend to be particularly blessed in this area, since 'Daddy' is usually one of the first, if not the very first word uttered by the little cherub.

Once the technique has been mastered, there will be no end to it. Not all the talking will make sense, and not all of it will be original, but it will be cute. Indeed, repetition and cuteness of expression are two of the defining features of any self-respecting toddler who wishes to consolidate his position within the family circle.

As time goes by, the extent of the toddler's vocabulary will be of great interest to the parents. Some of the words used will appear to have come out of the blue. The origin of other words will be all too obvious. Wherever the words have come from, the thrill on hearing a child begin to speak is, quite simply, enormous. The spoken word is a powerful tool at any stage in life. In the very early, formative stages, to hear a toddler having a bash at the English language brings great delight, and plays such a huge role in the development of an increasingly communicative relationship between parent and child.

Unwelcome Words

Swear words, just like any other words, will be picked up, stored, and brought out on a future occasion. To borrow an expression used by law enforcers, anything you say can and will be used as evidence. Sod's law dictates that the occasion will be highly embarrassing. Intensity is added to the embarrassment when the words are expressed in an appropriate context, suggesting that the toddler is fully cognizant of the import of the language, and of the power that can be obtained therewith.

Advanced Communications

Visual Clues

Adults may think that they can keep a straight face and not reveal what they are really thinking. They often succeed. Children, however, are not so good at hiding their feelings. Toddlers have absolutely no control over displaying their emotions. The best a toddler will achieve is a temporary suppression of the inner self. Generally, it only takes a few seconds for the face to give the game away.

The best example of this is to be seen after a little one has fallen over, or crashed into a wall, and then tried to hold back the tears. A few seconds, at most, may pass without any apparent sign of discomfort registering on the face. Then, the bottom lip begins to quiver, tears well up in the eyes, and a mixture of pain and embarrassment comes flooding forth.

Facial communication is not always this drastic. A simple frown is enough to demonstrate mild displeasure or perplexity. A delicately raised eyebrow reveals curiosity and surprise. These signs are all fairly basic, and within adult circles, they do not create much of an impact. When displayed by toddlers, such signs assume far greater significance. Again, they represent the early stages in the development of communication.

141

Visual techniques are as important as spoken and written techniques when it comes to learning how to put a message across.

The Writing's on the Wall

As soon as a child discovers how to hold a writing instrument, life becomes much more colourful. Assuming you quite like the way your house already looks, it will become extremely difficult to preserve the interior decor.

Literary Rules

1) All surfaces are considered suitable for inscription. Paper will suffice if it is provided; if not, then expect to come across evidence of creativity all over the house. Notable targets for defacement are prized pieces of antique furniture, table cloths, and walls – painted or papered, it makes no difference to the budding Monet. Our dining room wall, previously decorated solely in a delicate shade of rose white, now boasts all the colours of the visual spectrum. Fortunately, the damage inflicted on our Ducal dresser was minimal, and easily remedied. Otherwise, Georgina's future pocket money would have been held back until enough had been saved to pay for the services of a professional French polisher.

2) Pictures are equally as important as words. In the early stages, wonky matchstick cats and dogs may not tell a story, but they do represent how children view everyday sights around the home. For the time being, the letters C-A-T and D-O-G can wait, since pictorial displays are far more meaningful.

3) Squiggles are not to be sniffed at. Obviously, it would be a bit much to expect a toddler to commence writing perfectly formed letters right from the outset. First attempts generally comprise a mess of random lines. Perhaps the first

real sign of improvement is the development of the squiggle. Far more complex in shape than the straight line, the squiggle represents a real step forward in the child's attempt to express his artistic integrity. Hence, be impressed by this and by any other oddly shaped patterns.

4) Crayons can be interesting as a very basic first writing tool, but pencils are more interesting, coloured pencils are better still, and best of all are ink pens. Ballpoint pens, roller balls, felt tips, cartridge pens: they all have an amazing magnetism for little children. Perhaps children realize that they can add some measure of permanency to their scribbling; perhaps they are simply impressed by the boldness of the colours. Whatever the attraction, there really is no contest when it comes to choosing between a boring, legal pencil and an exciting, illicit ink pen.

5) In order not to become infuriated by what might seem like indiscriminate graffiti throughout the house, bear in mind that there are two very important activities going on here:

a) the child is learning a new skill. Remember how it feels to do something new?
b) the scribbles, however primitive, are a fundamental means of communication. Children can babble away for hours on end, to everyone's amusement, but sooner or later they will have to learn to master the written word. Literary composition must begin somewhere, and the dining room wall is probably as good a place as any.

So, try to regard the literature and the fine art as a way for the child to reach out to Mummy and Daddy, rather than as yet another form of mischief.

30

INTERACTING

Apart from quality one-on-one time with Mummy or Daddy, there is nothing that a toddler enjoys more than joining in with a crowd of fellow toddlers and running around like one of many headless chickens. Considering that there can be so many variations in character, it is amazing how the act of chasing after one another holds such universal appeal. Occasionally, a modicum of shyness may result in an initial spell of propping up the wall, or even in hiding behind Mummy. Even in these cases, the ice is generally melted by another little toddler daring to risk acquaintance. Similarity in disposition is not always to be welcomed, but in the context of a playschool or a nursery it can be a welcome relief to see one's own little darling happily playing along with all the other little darlings.

I tend to view nurseries as places where children can make friends and begin to influence people, rather than as a preliminary educational establishment. School comes along soon enough, and I do not see the need to start imposing the idea of academic education on children who still prefer and deserve to be treated as free spirits. Learning how to turn an empty washing-up liquid bottle into a rocket is about as clever as I would wish my children to get at such a tender, young, pre-school age. Social interaction is far more valuable than intellectual achievement at this time.

Sharing

Within any setting where children come up against each other, there are always little conflicts and differences of opinion. One of the most frequent reasons for disagreement is based on the idea of possession.

In the course of the last year, Georgina has found herself several times in the company of a delightful three-year-old cousin named Helena. On the first of these recent meetings, Georgina was not permitted to touch any of Helena's things. On the second occasion, prompted by an embarrassed mother, Helena very graciously provided a selection of toys for general sharing, to be kept separate from a second selection of items reserved for her own personal enjoyment. Needless to say, Georgina went straight for the forbidden pile. Prime target was a fluffy bunny called Mortimer, Helena's very own personal favourite toy companion. A bit of a scuffle ensued, after which the lines of demarcation were clearly redrawn. Mortimer of course, subsequently remained at Helena's side for the rest of the day.

The following conclusions suggest themselves:

1) certain toys seem more desirable than others, usually because they are already favoured by another child.
2) when sharing is not an attractive option, alternatives have to be established and accepted.
3) attaching a high value to material goods takes place at a very early age.

Television

In general, I regard children's viewing habits in much the same light as those of adults. The golden rule I apply is that anyone watching television should actively want to watch any specific programme. Watching for the sake of watching is unacceptable. Children should not be allowed, and parents should not allow themselves to fall into the trap of viewing without purpose. It reveals a hugely regrettable laziness that has afflicted the last few generations.

There are, of course, significant benefits that can be derived from watching television. Television may form part of the learning process. It may, equally, be greatly entertaining. On both counts, though, television should not be the main provider; it should act as a supplement. Allowing a child to sit in front of the box for hours on end is a dreadful relinquishment of parental responsibilities. If television is a person's biggest source of information, or his dominant form of entertainment, then there is clearly a great deal missing from that person's life.

Tubby or not Tubby?

Like it or not, one of the favourite children's programmes of the last few years has been *Teletubbies*. How long this will last remains to be seen. In my view, the shorter the better, but then, the programme is not designed to hold my attention. Frankly, I'm surprised that even my two-year-old daughter is impressed by them, but she is, and who am I to point her in a different direction? The attraction must be based on the combination of bold, primary colours, the inarticulate nature of their communication, and the repetitive nature of the features that fill out the rest of the program. Children seem to grasp at this sort of offering and keep hold of it until brighter and better programs come along. I trust it will not be too long before the Teletubbies disappear over the hill for good.

A Bit of a Barney

In contrast to the dreadful Dipsy and his friends, Barney comes across as a paragon of televisual virtue. Not only does this giant purple dinosaur stand out as an intelligent creature, he also maintains an inspiring boldness and a

146

marvellously engaging demeanour. American by nationality, Barney has a universal appeal, and captures the imagination of a fairly wide range of ages. Each programme contains music, dance, stories, adventures, and a whole host of other worthwhile features. The morals may be a bit simplistic, but the end song – 'I love you, you love me . . .' – more than makes up for any excess didacticism.

Musical Appreciation

It is widely accepted that babies enjoy lullabies and that little children like nursery rhymes set to music. What babies and toddlers really enjoy is probably the sound of a familiar, friendly voice. In the early stages of a child's development, the songs must be either catchy or soothing, or both. This will allow the child to latch on to key words and tunes, and to feel happy, safe, and comfortable within the musical world being created. From this point of view, lullabies and nursery rhymes are ideal. There comes a point, though, when these genres can seem tediously limiting. The loss of impact may occur gradually, and it is perhaps best demonstrated by a child who goes to sleep quickly without bothering to call for more.

Effectively, this process describes the child's changing tastes in music. The change can happen at a very young age. Whenever Georgina travels in the front seat of the car, she always gives the order 'Put radio on!' Note that she does not say 'Put nursery rhyme cassette on', which she could do quite easily. Nursery rhymes are old hat. Georgina's favourite these days is Janet Jackson, closely followed by All Saints. The words 'Never Ever' have become a rudimentary part of her vocabulary, and she has also learnt the chorus to 'Under the Bridge'. When nothing suitable comes forth on the airwaves, Georgina gives the order 'Radio off!' Georgina is still only two years old, take note.

Does Not Compute

Goggle Eyes

One of the many computer buzzwords popular these days is the term 'interaction'. Based on the regrettably increasing presence of computer technology within the lives of children today, the idea of interaction might seem valid. However, to a large extent, playing with a computer can be just another form of watching television. Even playing so-called interactive games involves a significant amount of staring at the screen. From the 'glued-to-the-box' point of view, personal computers are even worse than televisions in that the viewing takes place at extremely close range. In many cases, the most that you can say is that a child's eyes interact with the millions of pixels on the monitor. Other parts of the brain may also be engaged, but I am convinced that we are storing up mental and physical – more specifically, ocular – problems for ourselves as a nation.

Drawing the Line

Apart from this, there is also a very serious risk of missing out on any number of traditional games that provide at least as much, and probably a great deal more satisfying entertainment. Technology is fine as far as it goes, but we should not let it go too far. Certainly, technology should not be allowed to carry along with it our precious children in their formative years.

Learning can be a bit of a drag, at times, but the solution to this is never simply to sit a child down in front of a screen full of sixteen million colour variations, in between stereo speakers chucking out an extremely limited range of simulated noises. Multimedia machines have come on leaps and bounds in the past few years, but there is a time and a place for them. The time should be put off as long as possible, and the place most certainly is not in the nursery. Peer pressure may be applied, and schools may attempt to lead

148

our children down the slippery slope, but it really is time to stand up and say 'Oi, Microsoft, NO!!!'

Not All Progress is Good for the Age

I hesitate to say that computer games are absolutely a waste of life, but it would not take much for me to go so far. For the time being, let me merely underline the huge irony that exists behind the idea of computer interactivity. Computing may well involve a great deal of interacting with a screen, a keyboard, a mouse, and a joystick. It may well provide unlimited access to all computerized human knowledge. But, and this 'but' is enormous, how much fun can a child really get from playing with a few bits of basic hardware, and, how much knowledge can a child be expected to absorb? A diet based on chips is no better in the games room than it is in the dining room. Far better to present a child with a real-life pet mouse than with the latest ergonomically designed plastic rodent.

There is a virtual world constantly trying to creep in through the back door to our lives, yet there are so many simple, natural pleasures that are so much more stimulating, and which involve real-life participation. A traditional approach, I know, but I am not ashamed of it. Hats off to the clever boffins behind the multimedia age, by all means, but keep them away from my children. Lemmings may be encouraged elsewhere, but in my household, children will be warned to stay away from the abyss.

Learning the Rules

Learning to Move On

One of the fascinating aspects of a child's development is the contrast between the unpredictability of the timing involved in the different stages of the learning process, and the inevitablity about the way that each little milestone is quickly left behind in pursuit of the next.

A key moment in a child's life may be sudden and unexpected, or it may be the result of a long, patient and painful exercise. Depending on how the moment was arrived at, it will be welcomed by the parents with either amused excitement or with considerable relief. A mixture of these sentiments is frequently experienced.

Following on from the initial excitement of the breakthrough, some favoured activities will continue to be performed on a comparatively long-term basis, and a few may even become permanent habits. As a rule, the new-found skill that was so eagerly anticipated yesterday and for so many days previously, will, in turn, shortly become old hat.

Trial and Error

Games provide simple examples of the point in hand. However precisely you may verbalize the instructions for a game, and however avid the apparent level of interest, a toddler will plainly not learn to play a game only by listening. Equally, at such a tender young age, asking the toddler to read the blurb on the inside of the box is asking just a little too much. Watching an adult or an older child may provide some clues, but this is only a starting point. The only way to really learn is through active participation. The child must be encouraged to get stuck in, and to make his or her own sense of the action. An understanding of the object of the game will then be arrived at through a series of repeated errors and an appreciation of the parents' reaction to those errors.

Having finally grasped the essentials, the child will play along happily for some time before realizing that it is now time to go off again in search of another game. Once a child has mastered any game or activity, the level of interest therein will reach a saturation point, and it will be time to move on. A new challenge awaits just around every corner.

Pairing Off

A specific example might be a game of pairs, where the object of the game is to turn over a picture card, and then to turn over another identical card. Having found a pair, the two cards can then be placed on a separate pile, to be counted up at the end of the game. To begin with, the child will want to pick up the cards in random fashion, chew them, throw them underneath the sofa, and then wander off in search of something more interesting. Several repeat performances will ensue until, one day, the penny will begin to drop. For some inexplicable reason, the child will seem to suddenly understand that a boat goes with a boat, or that two apples go jolly nicely together, or, that having found and identified a ball, it might be fun to try and find another ball.

Imagination/Concentration/Similarity

There are, of course, many possible reasons why success should happen on any one day. As I see things, the following are the most prominent possibilities:

1) The child will become bored of playing a game that has no obvious point of interest other than to look at pictures, and will consequently invite the imagination to play an increasing role in the game each time it is played, up until the point of comprehension.
2) There is a potential for a child's concentration span to increase as each day goes by. Consequently, an activity that seems tedious or convoluted one day may seem interesting and simple the next.
3) On a deeper level, the child gradually succumbs to an impulsive desire to bring some sense of order to life. Establishing a likeness between two previously disparate objects is the humblest beginning of such a quest.

151

Whatever the explanation, the child's happiness at discovering how to do something, and, more to the point, how to do something that is rewarded with praise, is matched only by the parent's joy at witnessing the next measurable stage in the child's intellectual growth.

31

SECOND THOUGHTS

The early stages of parenthood may have seemed extremely difficult. The pregnancy may have been problematic; the labour long, drawn-out, and complicated; and the subsequent early stages considerably hard work. The sound of crying may have driven you up the wall. Baby tricks, however innocent and harmless, may have been played on you just once too often for you to maintain soundness of mind.

But, let's face it, Daddy, you did it! With the help of the mother, you summoned baby into the world, taught baby to eat, sleep, and generally to begin the process of becoming a reasonable human being. You know how to dodge the spoonful of Organix when it gets flicked your way, you know all the words to all of the nursery rhymes once again, and you feel good, because your own life has changed hugely. You even have the smirk to prove it, for it has all been marvellous. So, why would you not want to do it all over again?

Maybe things were not that great, after all. Maybe the fears that you had originally have never quite been dispelled. Alternatively, maybe everything is so perfect that you do not wish to risk failing to match the same standards next time around. Maybe, just maybe, your gut reaction is to say 'No' to more, without really understanding why. You just think that one is fine, and that two, for whatever reason, would be a mistake.

During the early stages of fatherhood, you may well have cause to wonder first 'Was it all worth it?' and then 'Is it worth doing again?' An affirmative answer to the first question should hopefully be quick in coming. As for the second question, this may take longer.

I can vividly remember telling a colleague in the office that although I was really glad that I had been through the whole experience once, I did not think that I would be repeating the exercise. At the time, I was as definite as I had ever been about anything. My colleague suggested that in time, my views might change, but I would have no truck with that. Time does indeed change things, and after about a year into the life of our first child, I was beginning to think that perhaps it would be a good idea to have a bash at making number two. Whilst, earlier on, any number of circumstances and potential circumstances could have swayed me either way, I became convinced that a second child would be absolutely delightful.

Having undergone this significant change of heart, I began to feel that I was merely falling in line with the commands of Nature. Along with a heartfelt desire to be involved in another wonderful act of sharing, I believe that I also indulged myself in a wish to help populate the earth with my own progeny. The male ego receives a tremendous boost whenever you hear that your seed has prospered in a fertile environment. Knowledge of a second baby on the way confirmed that the first had not been a fluke. Moreover, everything simply seemed right.

Looking back, with numbers one and two both bringing great joy into the family, I now know that submitting to my paternal instincts was, on both occasions, a sensationally good decision. I have learnt that you do not need to keep an open mind all of the time. The key to it all is getting your timing right.

More to Life Than This?

When you become a parent for the first time round, you will probably be happy to talk to almost anyone about almost anything related to babies. Unless there is a delay of many years between the first and the second, by the time the second is born, you may well be a bit more reticent about the topic. One of the main reasons for this is that having fully enjoyed the euphoria brought on the first time round, you will by now have come to realize that babies are not the only interest in life. If they are, then you could find yourself regretting it for a number of different reasons. Up to a certain point, basing your life around bringing up children may be necessary and even desirable, but there should always be room for at least one or two more adult pursuits. Life would be frightfully limited otherwise.

The birth of the second baby and any further babies should, of course, still bring great joy to all involved, especially the parents. By concentrating too hard on maintaining non-baby interests and pursuits, simply to give an impression of being well-rounded and independent, there is a potential danger. This danger involves missing out on the enjoyment of another round of highly justifiable extremes of positive emotion. The father, especially, may suffer the dilemma of wanting to love the new baby dearly, but feeling restrained by a desire not to be seen to be completely besotted with the whole child-rearing process. Each man must resolve this potential conflict for himself.

The same scenario could apply equally well to mothers. In most cases, though, any negative feelings are diminished by the immediate proximity of the new-born baby. It would take a very hard woman to be more concerned with anything other than the baby, especially when breast-feeding.

Mixed Emotions

My own initial reactions were incredibly mixed. In the lead-up to the birth, I had felt delight at the prospect of becoming a father again, but I also experienced some feelings of trepidation. On the positive side, I remembered how wonderful and exciting the first birth had been, and I largely

155

expected the second birth to follow a similar pattern. Seeing your own child being born is one of the most exhilarating, albeit mentally draining experiences that you could ever hope to enjoy. Being present at the very beginning of a new creation is one of the rarest of rare privileges in life.

On a slightly less ethereal level, I was looking forward to seeing Angela relieved of her burden, however treasured the load was. I was also looking forward to being able to announce to family and friends that I was, once again, the proud father of a new baby. With our first child being a girl, I had admitted that I was hoping, at least just a little bit, for a boy the second time around. The suspense involved in not knowing the sex of the unborn child was really quite exciting.

Perhaps most important of all, I was eagerly anticipating the arrival of the baby, in order that I might begin to love the newest member of my family. You can feel fondly towards the unborn child contained within the mother's 'bump', but a full, loving relationship can only really be established once the little being has finally left the womb, and can be seen and held.

In contrast to these positive feelings, I also experienced some degree of anxiety. My main concern was that I would not be able to feel and show the same level of affection for the second child as I had done for the first. Moreover, I was happy with the way things already were, and I was a little worried that the new arrival might disturb things for the worse. With our first child approaching the age of two, I was starting to feel relieved that the normal hardships that arise in the course of bringing up a baby had, by and large, now been phased out. Here we were, about to embark on a repeat of all those hardships, and probably to suffer some new ones, to boot. Having only recently recaptured some sense of individuality, I was now, once again, about to be restrained by the trappings and demands involved in bringing up another baby.

Clearly, the feelings stacked up on both sides. Overall, I can confidently say that the positives outweighed the negatives, and I tend to attribute this to the charms of my baby son, rather than to my own system of values. The only conclusion I can draw from this is that in matters of such great importance, conflicting thoughts and emotions will always come to the fore. Making choices, and learning to live with them, is what life is all about.

Now that we have two young children, evenings just disappear. I can no longer sit and read *The Times* as Angela goes upstairs to lay the baby down for the night. Our first is now a toddler who needs at least ten books to be read to her, preferably ending up with the complete *Mother Goose* compendium of nursery rhymes. Our second is still very much a baby. Hence, both our children simultaneously require individual attention. Unless Granny comes to stay, taking a back seat is no longer an option. Of course, I knew that having a second would force me into action. Perhaps this was a motivating factor in deciding to have a second child. If only on a subconscious level, I'm sure I must have wanted to live up to my responsibilities, and to perform my share of the domestic tasks.

Moving Up the Pecking Order

So far, I have approached the subject of increasing the flock solely from a parental viewpoint. There is also much to be gained from considering things from a child's perspective.

A first child's reactions to the presence of a new baby can be quite fascinating, particularly if the first child is also still very young. Within our family, the interest has centred around the interaction between a twenty-two-month-old toddler and a new baby. Thankfully, our toddler seemed delighted to welcome the new baby home. Indeed, it was not long before Georgina started trying to shower the baby with kisses. This was followed up by attempts to bear-hug the baby, and subsequent expressions of approval. We lost count of the number of times we heard Georgina say the words 'Nice baby'. This came out in such a wonderfully cute, childlike way, yet in a style that was so reminiscent of the kind of sentiments more usually expressed by adults.

However, the kisses and the attempted hugs were not the only expressions of interest exhibited by our toddler. The main alternative was for Georgina to grab hold of the side of the Moses basket and to shake it with all her might. Other less than welcome actions included stealing the baby's cuddly toys, patting the baby on the head, and, more worryingly, attempting to scratch the baby's face.

In both cases, Georgina was clearly showing a willingness to include the new baby within her own little world. The contrast between the different actions exhibited seemed to demonstrate, quite starkly, the duality of the human condition. This might sound quite a grandiose explanation for what you may consider to be a perfectly normal sequence of events. As a would-be child psychologist, I feel fully justified in believing that children reveal a lot about basic humanity.

Shifting Loyalties

In many cases, the first child will be quite happy to allow Mummy to go into hospital to have a new baby, but will react badly on her return. Rather than feeling pleased at having Mummy back, the child may keep Mummy at a distance, and may even show some animosity towards her. If Granny has been looking after the child at home, then Granny may well take the place of Mummy in the child's affections. Usually, this scenario does not last for long. As for Daddy, there is apparently limitless potential for increased bonding with the older child. Since Mummy picks up the blame for going away on unauthorized leave, Daddy may well be rewarded with double the usual level of affection.

32

SECOND INNINGS

To a certain extent, having a second child allows you to compensate for any experiences that were missed out on the first time. Whilst I believe, on the whole, that Angela and I made a decent fist of bringing our first child into the world, there were undoubtedly important aspects of babyhood that slipped by unnoticed at the time.

Even though women's cricket does take place, a cricket-loving father always hopes for a boy, in order to pass on his appreciation for and experience of the game. By no means do I dare to suggest that having a girl first was a mistake, or even that the later arrival of a boy was an improvement. I merely hazard a guess that little Devon will be more likely to share his father's passion for the game even more comprehensively than his big sister will.

Net Gain

There is a tradition within Haste Hill Cricket Club that whenever a player becomes a father during the winter nets season, attendance at the first nets session after delivery is compulsory. Georgina was born in the wrong season to allow me to take part in this ritual, but Devon was born in February, midway through the pre-season preparations. At one stage, it was touch and go, since nets were due to happen two days after the birth. Then, on the day in question, Angela decided that one more night in hospital would be a good idea. Whilst I did not actively encourage her to stay in hospital one more night, I told her that even though I would miss her terribly, I thought it was the right decision. Bingo! Before you could say 'Christopher Martin-Jenkins', I was round the M25, along the lanes running through Rickmansworth and Northwood, and arriving excitedly at the indoor cricket school. There I stood, a fully committed member of the Haste Hill Proud Fathers' Club, Gray Nicolls in hand, ready to adopt my favourite stance in the nets.

Missed Chances and Oversights

When Georgina was born, I neglected my duty in two specific matters. First, I failed to see that she was correctly attired for the official family portrait. Second, I overlooked my obligation to give her some early catching practice. Simple oversights, you might feel, but as Lord MacLaurin of Tesco and the English Cricket Board says, 'Image is crucial'; and, as almost every commentator around says, 'Catches win matches'.

So, when Devon was born, I resolved not to make the same slip-ups twice. For Devon's official family picture, I ensured that he was immaculately turned out in a pristine set of whites. Even Alec Stewart would have looked untidy beside our Devon.

As for the catching practice, as soon as Devon took possession of his Moses basket, I tossed a cricket ball at him over and over again. This not only gave him the chance to show how good his hands were, but also provided him with a first smell of leather. Both these features should ensure that Devon has a fine future in the game.

Caribbean Concerns

Devon will, at some stage, have to resolve another highly important issue. With one English parent and one Jamaican, our son will inevitably have to tackle the Norman Tebbit cricket test. As far as I am concerned, I would be happy for him to play for either England or the West Indies. If current standards prevail, both teams could do with some strengthening in the batting line-up. Both teams are also short of a world-class bowler. Hence, with a little application, Devon could be knocking on the doors of two sets of selectors in about eighteen years' time.

In order not to make Georgina feel left out, I arranged some daily sessions with her, listening to the test match commentary during the recent series in the Caribbean. Remembering how perceptive she had been over a year ago in citing Graeme Hick as a top batsman, I now decided to give Georgina another chance to shine. Her ability to recite the respective batting line-ups of the two teams was quite brilliant. Names such as Ramprakash, Ramnarine, and Chanderpaul were rattled off with consummate ease. Great-uncle Richie had obviously taught her well.

For her *pièce de resistance*, Georgina then came out with the astonishingly good command: 'Brian Lara; GET OUT!' This was accompanied by the pointing of the index finger of the right hand, to signify dismissal. Finally, she let out a chuckle of delight. If there was any room left for doubt over how *she* felt about the Tebbit test, the follow-up offered confirmation: 'Alec Stewart; STAY IN.' Overall, a remarkable performance. Perhaps I should take another look at women's cricket.

33

SPECIAL RELATIONSHIPS

It is often claimed that there is a special relationship between father and daughter, and an equally special one between mother and son. But then, such a division of partiality is far too much of an over-simplification. If relationships are so straightforward, then why do women spend hours and hours on the telephone to their mothers? Furthermore, why do so many fathers take such obvious delight in exclaiming 'That's my boy', on seeing even the slightest demonstration of Bothamesque cricketing ability? Clearly, the issue is not so clear-cut. There is huge scope for all sorts of relationships to arise out of diverse circumstances and events.

Nevertheless, patterns of preference can be allowed, and even encouraged to develop from a very early stage. At the baby stage, it might seem as if there should be no grounds for preferences, but there is indeed a potential for male and female babies to inspire different feelings in mothers and fathers. The following suggests contrasting ways in which a father is likely to relate to his offspring.

Sugar and Spice

A baby girl may look sweet in pretty dresses and ribbons, and will thus charm her Daddy in a highly feminine way. She may seem like a miniature version of her mother. The father will then be doubly delighted in having two delectable females in the family; a beautiful daughter to go with a beautiful wife. There is, of course, always the risk of Daddy's little princess behaving like a tomboy. Left unchecked, this might just cause some regret. The best cure would seem to be the presentation of a Barbie doll at the earliest opportunity.

On those rare occasions when the sun disappears behind a cloud, the little girl's crying will be regarded as only to be expected from a female.

Puppy Dogs' Tails

In contrast, a baby boy may cut a dash in a fashion that is more handsome than pretty. The father may well regard his son as being a welcome chip off the old block: a manly extension of himself. Taken to an extreme, the father might even try to project his own masculinity (real or desired) onto the little man-child.

Whilst girls are not allowed to thump their daddies, rough and tumble is simply fair game between boys and men. Girls are supposed to offer hugs. Boys are allowed to be little thugs. In Next Generation *terms, consider the immense bonding between Lieutenant Commander Worf and his son Alexander, a future Klingon warrior in the making. Whilst crying may be acceptable in infancy, and tolerated for a few moments in early boyhood, it will need to be phased out in later life.*

Feel free to argue with my own gross over-simplification, but from personal experience I suggest that a father is likely to feel delicate, doting thoughts about his sweet little daughter, and hardy, man-to-man empathy with his little bruiser of a son. This is not to say that I rate children of one sex any more highly than those of the other. Girls and boys simply possess different kinds of equally endearing characteristics, and inspire equally loving degrees of admiration. Bonding can be special, regardless of biological specification.

163

Of course, you can argue until the cows come home about the relative appeals of baby girls and baby boys. I do not offer a preference; first, because such a choice would be likely to upset my second favourite when she or he is ready to read this book; second, because I do not have to. I am completely happy having both a girl and a boy, and there is no real benefit in trying to play one off against the other. In times to come, Devon might play a more exquisite cover drive, but Georgina might make a superior chicken and mushroom pie. What would be the point in trying to choose between the two?

34

WORMHOLES AND RISKS

Approaching parenthood might feel like being on the edge of your own private wormhole. Wormholes, as all good *Star Trek* followers will know, are spatial rifts that allow travel to another section of the galaxy at normally inconceivable speeds. They appear to be full of mystery, and perhaps fragile in their existence; certainly they are transitory. Above all, they offer a passage through to another state of being; to another time and space where things will be different. Having arrived on the other side of the wormhole, you will find yourself light years from your previous location.

This seems to depict a number of the key aspects of becoming parents. Circumstances will change drastically. A return to the previous state is highly unlikely, even if it is to be desired. If at all possible, a return to normality will take years. As in the case of *Star Trek Voyager*, the journey is destined to last a lifetime. By the time that lifetime has passed, the original conditions will probably no longer exist anyway.

The wormhole in *Deep Space Nine* is not only a means of conveyance from one physical location to another, it is also a place of tremendous spiritual significance. Submitting to the instinctive call to procreate is the same as entering the wormhole, in that it demands trust in the spiritual forces and the physical realities that dominate our lives. Of course, there are risks. Prospective parents may be unsettled by so many potential dangers and uncertainties. Nevertheless, overriding all of the risks there is a sense of destiny that must be fulfilled. Generation after generation, we are compelled to rise to the challenge of ensuring the continuity of our existence.

So, be prepared to enter the wormhole. A move from the Alpha Quadrant to the Gamma Quadrant may seem scary, and at times the fear may prove to be justified. Overall, though, it will be a hugely rewarding adventure. The experiences will be rich and varied, fascinating and enlightening. The cultures you will encounter will be like nothing you have experienced before. Above all, entering a wormhole, just like choosing to become parents, entails making an inspired choice for the future. The choice may seem like a gamble, but then, life is not confined to certainties. The element of risk must be measured against what you consider you have to lose. Looking at this another way, more might be lost by choosing not to take the plunge.

Having children is a marvellous way of prospering in life. Make it so.

Index 1: BABY TALK

Index 2: CRICKET

Index 3: STAR TREK

Index 4: PEOPLE AND PLACES